ESSAYS ON SCARBOROUGH HISTORY

compiled by

Alan Whitworth

First Published in 2006 by
Heritage House Press
An Imprint of
F.J. Blissett & Co Ltd.
Roslin Road,
London. W3 8DH.

For current information on other titles and services provided through Heritage House Press, please contact:

Heritage House Press.
19 South Ridge,
Kippax.
Leeds. LS25 7NE.
Tel: 0113 286 0819.
E-mail: mmikethebook@aol.com

ISBN: 1-905912-00-5

Printed in the UK By Blissetts Digital

CONTENTS

Chapter:

Acknowledgements

I should like to take this opportunity of thanking the many who have contributed to this book in so many different ways; in particular I owe a debt of gratitude to Scarborough Local History Library for allowing publication of the Rowntree material and to Jean Wallington for editing the original work; also to the Scarborough Antiques & Collectors Centre, St. Nicholas Cliff for their help in finding illustrations.

On the production side, I should like to thank Howard Bicknell for his layout and design, and finally Mike Parsons, of Heritage House Press, for his faith in publishing this volume, hopefully the first of a series on essays in Scarborough history.

Introduction

THEY SAY VARIETY IS THE SPICE OF LIFE. In this volume of essays on Scarborough history, there is a plentiful diversity of material.

Obviously the town's maritime tradition is reflected in the chapter on shipwrecks, as well as the one on the lifeboats which provide an essential service to the former.

Another aspect of its commercial history is recorded in the story of Rowntree's department store, now long since gone but which played a large part in the life of Scarborough for so many years.

Water of a different kind is mentioned in a chapter on the water supply of the town, its wells and reservoirs – which subject neatly reminds me of another beverage discussed in the ensuing pages, ale and the public houses and inns of the town: liquid of another sort, but not necessarily as good for your health as the spa waters of Scarborough!

Terra firma is represented in the brief chapter on the history of street names and in a lengthier piece about the tramways of the town, such an essential mode of transport necessary for the town's growth in the nineteenth century.

All in all an impressive assortment of subjects which I hope the reader will enjoy.

Alan Whitworth
August 2006

Chapter 1

Some Brief Notes on Scarborough Street Names

IN PREVIOUS CENTURIES, many of the old streets in the town of Scarborough took their names from persons living in the immediate neighbourhood. Globe Street was formerly called Stockdale Street, after a person of that name who resided in the house later known as the *Old Globe Inn*. Dog and Duck Lane, we are informed, obtained its name from a person called 'Doggy' Duck, who kept a barking dog there. Parkin's Lane, a narrow passage leading into Quay Street, was named after Mr. Parkin, an eminent sail maker, who resided there. Potter's Lane, leading from Castlegate to the Castle Hill, probably arose through Mr. Christopher Potter and others of that name residing in it. Princess Lane formerly went by the name of Willie Endick's Lane, after a blacksmith who had a forge there.

Quay Street was commonly called Quay End. Princess Street was called the Saturday Market – the old Market Cross is still to be seen near the conduit; in 1776 the Martinmass Fair was held in that locality. Queen Street was known as the Beast Market, and in even more ancient days as Blackfriar Gate. Pen's Back Lane, near Dean Street, has through time been changed to Penny Black Lane.

Newborough Street is mentioned by Leland (c. 1506-52), in reference to Newburg or Newborrow Gate (Figure 1). The same may be said of Auborough Street, as Aldeburg Gate. Newborough Street, previous to the Market Hall being erected, was the Thursday Market. Pots, glass, and earthenware were dis-

Fig. 1: Newborough Gate

played from the Bar to St. Nicholas Street; stalls with every kind of merchandise were ranged on each side of the street down to St. Helen's Square, which was the Meat Market. The Pig Market was held in front of the Theatre, in Tanner Street, now called St. Thomas Street. King Street was called Elderberry Lane, and was also known as Apple Market, where apples, pears, and other fruits were sold in 'a penny loaf heap' it is said to have been named King Street, it being in a line with Queen Street, by desire of Mr. John Hornsey, who had an academy there.

Mr. Stephen Wharton caused King Street Steps to be made to the Sands, his property being between this boundary and Bland's Cliff – these steps were of great assistance to the public, as the road previously presented a very rugged descent to the shore.

Huntriss Row was formerly called Harding's Walk; a Mr. Harding resided in a dwelling where the Assembly Rooms were later erected. The name was changed by a noted builder, Mr. Jonathan Huntriss, who began to erect the row of buildings on the

East side, intending to reside with his family in the stone building in the centre.

Aberdeen Walk was formerly called Bull Lane, and Aberdeen Terrace stands on the site of Mr. Hick's nursery garden, at the bottom of which it was possible to shoot snipe and, one assumes, other game birds.

The Ropery, or Workhouse Lane, was so called because the Workhouse entrance was there, and Wharton's Ropery was also in the neighbourhood, which extended nearly the length of North Street. Workhouse Lane is now called Waterhouse Lane, from under the archway of the Old Coffee House to the house formerly belonging to Mr. Dennis; and the narrow passage leading into Newborough used to be called Liddle's Lane.

Dumple Street was called Dunpole Street. Long Westgate was formerly called the King's Highway.

The Banks, as they were called, formed part of Castlegate; a place called Clark's Bank was in front of a house belonging to Mrs. Clark, and which was later occupied for many years by Mrs. Isabella Moffatt, a greengrocer, who had a shop at the entrance to the old Shambles. The Castle Crescent is built on the bank above named, and Paradise Row on the site of Mrs. Clark's house. Frazier's Bank was situated between Potter Lane and the Borough Bank. Willie and Jenny Frazier occupied this site, and had a garden there. It was then occupied by Joseph Waterworth, and after him, by William Short and still retains the name of Short's Garden.

The highest house in Castlegate was long occupied by Mr. Robert Cooke, and his son Robert; Mr. Cooke being at one time Overseer of the Poor. A story is told how he once called upon a person named Andrew Kipper to collect the rates, but Mr. Kipper refused to pay them without a receipt. Mr. Cooke, being somewhat eccentric, gave him a receipt as follows: *Andrew Kipp, a crafty knave, a receipt from me he'd have, 'twas but for a simple groat, I care not if all the town knows, I neither drink nor smoke, witness my hand ROBERT COOKE.*

Grey Friars Street is mentioned in the sixteenth century. Friars Entry marks the site of the Dominican house founded in 1252. In 1298 the order received permission to make a street towards their church within the town wall. Black Friar Gate, now Queen Street, is mentioned in the year 1611.

Fig. 2: A corner of Foreshore Road below the Castle Walls

Fig. 3: North Marine Road.

The remains of the old Market Cross showing the Well-House.

Chapter 2

Notes on Scarborough's
Ancient Water Supply

THE GRANT OF A WELL in a place called *Guildhusclif*, a hill near Falsgrave, was confirmed by the burgesses of Scarborough, in the thirteenth year of the reign of Edward II (1319-20), for the purpose of making an aqueduct to the Priory of the Dominican Friars. This aqueduct afterwards supplied the various water conduits in the town. Some additional springs in the same vicinity were later taken in, and the Corporation obtained a lease from the late Joseph Denison, Esq., for a certain portion of the spring near Stone Hags, at the further end of Seamer Lane, and the three conduits, known as the High Conduit, the Middle Conduit, in Sepulchre Street, and the Low Conduit, near Princess Street, were supplied from this source.

The stone conduits of the Franciscan friars were eventually replaced by lead pipes, which were possibly passed inside them, a technique found elsewhere in England. The minutes of Scarborough Corporation indicate that the improvements were made during the first half of the seventeenth century. The lead pipes ran along Falsgrave Road, or in the King's Close, which lay between Falsgrave Road and Londesborough Road. In 1628 Scarborough Corporation laid down that '. . . *every inhabitant shall fynd a sufficient laboring man to bare and dig upp the conduit pipes from Newborough Gate to the conduit head and to cover it agayne, and for want of such labourer to pay every tyme 6d to the sayd work.*'

Later three cisterns were erected at each of the Conduits so that water levels could be built up in times of light use and so supply water during times of heavy use. In 1634 a decree commanded that the Middle Conduit should be covered over with a locked trap door to be opened only between six o'clock in the morning and six in the evening.

By the nineteenth century, the Low, Middle and Upper Conduits and their channels were insufficient to provide the water for Scarborough and 'scenes of disorder, contention, turmoil, trouble and often fights' were reported as inhabitants crowded round the troughs to draw water.

Another important early source of water for the townspeople of Scarborough was the water course known as the Damyot, or Damgeth, which rose in Albemarle Crescent and flowed north of Westborough, turning south near St. Sepulchre Street before entering the sea near the Lifeboat House. The origin of the name may have come from the Old Norse *dammr*, meaning dam, and *geyt*, gushing spring or stream, and may be associated with the mill operated by Reginald the Miller in the thirteenth century, who gave land on either side of the Damyot near the cemetery of the Church of the Holy Sepulchre to *the Commonality of Scardburgh, to support the friars dwelling and serving God there.*

The stream has run in a culvert since the early nineteenth century.

Before the water was supplied to Scarborough, the population was in the habit of visiting two large springs on the South Sands – the Mill Beck and Peasholme (Figure 1) – or any other running stream.

There were many wells in the town that are but little regarded now.

In the year 1788, the 29th Regiment was housed in Scarborough Barracks. Down in the Castle Holmes, beneath the cliff, opposite the coble landing, there was a fine spring, and the regiment placed two casks for the water, which remained useful for many years.

Fig. 1: Peasholme Beck running through the Glen

Following the great Siege of Scarborough, an account of the damages sustained by the town during that conflict was presented to the House of Commons in November 1646 by Sir Matthew Boynton, Bart, which included mention that damage was done by the *'spoiling of their Conduit, which brought water in leaden pipes to the Towne, a mile from thence, by pulling up and break- ing the pipes.'* The value of the losses was given as £200, presum- ably for replacing the conduit pipes. However, it is not clear whether this amount was ever paid or the leaden pipes repaired.

Under an arched vault in the castle yard, near the ruins of an ancient chapel, there is a reservoir called the Lady's Well, supposedly consecrated, in more devout days, to the Virgin Mary. It is difficult, using geographical principles, to determine its source, as the nearest adjacent land of equal, or greater, elevation, is more than a mile distant and with which it does not now appear to have the least communication.

The following circumstance is offered as a solution to the conundrum, and it carries with it a great deal of plausibility. It is said that the engineer who superintended the barracks and other military works, about the year 1746, ordered the workmen to dig a circular trench round the reservoir in order to trace the source. They discovered several subterranean drains or channels which appeared to have been made for the purpose of conduiting the rainwater that fell upon the area of the Castle Hill.

This reservoir, when filled, contained about forty tons of water, which was said to be very clear, and has been found in tests to weigh lighter by one ounce per gallon than any other water in the vicinity.

The water from this source was the object of an amusing circumstance many years ago involving some strangers to Scarborough: The late master of the Coffee House (Mr. William Cockerill), a person of great humour and ingenuity, having often been asked by the company who were staying at his house to introduce Bristol water to his table, substituted the castle water in its place. The deception was carried out with great dexterity. The wax on the corks bore the impression of the Bristol seal. He claimed it was freshly imported every season, guaranteed from the fountainhead. The 'connoisseurs' pronounced it genuine.

But the ingenuity of the proprietor failed him at an unguarded moment. He had, in convivial company, taken too much wine. In the confusion of his intoxication he applied the 'Bristol' seal to a bottle of sherry which was hastily sent up to the table even before the wax had time to cool.

This unlucky circumstance led to his discovery; and the master of the Coffee House not only received a severe reprimand for the imposture, but also was obliged ever after to supply the water *gratis*. No doubt, as its reputation was established and the demand considerable, he lost a pretty penny as the result of his misplaced sense of humour!

At the dawn of the nineteenth century, Scarborough Corporation considered a variety of schemes to improve and increase the supply of water to the town. Initially Robert King, of Pickering, surveyor, was asked for advice on improving the water system. It was King who surveyed Washington DC from 1797 to 1803.

Later, the pioneer geologist William Smith recommended that 'the largest covered reservoir in England' be dug in what is now Chapman's Yard in Waterhouse Lane. This reservoir was capable of containing 4,000 hogsheads of water.

The reservoir occupied the ground near which the old Workhouse stood, with the House of Correction at the back, and which once formed a part of the range of buildings and stables behind the Temperance Hall, in North Street.

While the workmen were excavating the ground for the reservoir, a portion of a once 'fair and spacious' church was exposed to view, and several entire skeletons were dug up, but no inscriptions were discovered. An antique piece of cutlery, a spur, etc., were also found, and deposited in the Museum.

The water was conducted into the town in cast-iron pipes, laid down in 1820, and completed in 1828.

In modern times, the improvement of Scarborough's water supply was spurred on by the increase in population. Between the census of 1821 and that of 1841 Scarborough's resident population grew from 8,188 to 9,503 – an increase of only 16%. However, by 1861, it had grown to 17,284, an increase of nearly 82%. Nothing like this expansion had ever occurred before. It was so remarkable that those who summarised the Census Returns of 1861 felt obliged to offer an explanation. In the words of their Report: 'The increase of population in Scarborough is attributed to the extension of railway communication and improvements in the town, which is resorted to as a watering-place during the season.'

However, the romance of the railways which arrived in the summer of 1845, has obscured the prosaic truth, that the prosperity of mid-Victorian Scarborough owed at least as much to the steam water pump as it did to the steam locomotive. In fact, the Scarborough Water Act of 1845, the most important improvement to the amenities of the town, was as vital to its future as the contemporary York-Scarborough Railway Act.

The Scarborough Waterworks Company was founded in 1844 by John Woodall and other local business and property owners. Suspicions that public interest would be sacrificed in favour of the interests of shareholders were allayed by undertakings from Woodall and his associates being written into the Act passed the following year. In return for a monopoly of supplying water to Scarborough and Falsgrave, the Company agreed to limits on charges to private homes and guaranteed that the three public conduits would remain open for free domestic use every day from 6 am to 9 pm. As a result, the Act gave the Company control of the supply pipes, the Workhouse Yard reservoir and all the existing sources of water in Falsgrave, Stoney Haggs, Staxton, Flixton and Cayton.

Yet none of these changes would have added one drop of water to the town's inadequate supply without the introduction of Trevithick's steam pumps at Cayton Bay in 1872. Here, each day, 400,000 gallons of water were lifted about 100 feet by Cornish-style steam engines to a reservoir at Osgodby Bank Top, capable of holding a million gallons, and from there conveyed by water mains along the line of Filey Road into Scarborough itself.

From here on nearly every householder was assured of a reliable flow of clean water for baths, closets, kitchens and laundries, while every area, not only those close to the fixed water points of the old town, could become residential. In particular, Scarborough could now expand outwards from its southern and western perimeters. From 1845 onwards several hotels and lodging houses were advertising that they had 'plenty of good water'.

Such was the increasing demand for water that in 1853 a new steam pump, nearly twice as powerful as its predecessor, was installed at the Cayton Cliff Works. Two years later, the old reservoir at Seacliff was abandoned in favour of one at Osgodby Top with four times its capacity.

In 1884 an additional water works was built at Irton, where two large beam-engine pumps were capable of drawing 1,250,000 gallons of water a day from the 428 feet well to a reservoir at the summit of Oliver's Mount.

*A street scene in busy Scarborough
in the first decade of the twentieth century.*

Chapter 3

The Early Trams and Buses of Scarborough

T HE PROVISION AND MAINTENANCE of public transport is essential to the growth and development of any town or city. Private vehicles in large numbers clog up and prohibit the free flow of traffic in streets and roads. The pollution they emit is harmful to buildings and people alike and so it is proper that they should be restricted. But if a local authority is to restrict access to private vehicles, it must make provision for public transport to carry the occupants of those private vehicles it has put off the roads to chosen destinations whether for work or play.

Also, there are many sections of the community that cannot or prefer not to own and operate a private vehicle. A local authority has a duty to provide alternative means of transportation for these people.

In the late-Victorian and early-Edwardian era, when the motor car was in its infancy but rapidly gaining a foothold in the public consciousness and beginning to create its own unique problems, our forefathers made provision to restrict their spread by the establishment of a public transport system which, at the time, was the envy of the world.

Today with our interest in nostalgia, early cars, old buses and trams are key exhibits to be visited in museums and are among the most popular of visitor attractions. Indeed, in places where the latter have been retained or brought back into service, such as Blackpool, they are an asset to the town.

In many towns and cities today, as fossil fuel and transport issues becomes a problem and other sources of both are required, designers and planners are often turning to the older methods of transportation for ideas. Trams are making a come-back in some towns, trolley buses are being re-introduced, all in the name of progress, but essentially because many of these proved successful in the past and could not really be beaten for economy and performance.

In Scarborough, interestingly, the early tramcars were not popular and the era of the tramway was short-lived (Figure 1). Indeed, initial applications to set up a tramway system met much opposition. The first application came in April 1896, when the Corporation Streets and Buildings Committee was asked to consider a route to be funded from the South Foreshore Road to

Fig. 1: Tramcar No. 27, originally built in 1903 and acquired in 1926 from Ipswich Corporation Tramways. It carried 50 passengers and was powered by two 25hp motors

Peasholm via the Marine Drive, then still unmade. This was refused. After several further unsuccessful applications, which were submitted almost annually by different syndicates, the Town Council was finally persuaded of the desirability of a tramway in the year 1901 at the very end of Queen Victoria's reign.

The task of creating a tramway system was given to a Mr. Swinton, of Westminster, London. He duly appeared before the Corporation with his plans, and a Bill to construct and work the tramway system was laid before Parliament in 1902. Royal Assent was given on 23 June of that year.

The *Scarborough Tramways Act* authorised 3 miles and 20 chains of double track to be constructed and 3 miles and 23 chains of single track. The system was to be built within the span of two years, except for a section along Marine Drive, which was to be constructed in a single year when Marine Drive itself was made. Eventually, Marine Drive was completed in 1908 but no track was ever laid (Figure 2). A combination of its exposed position,

Fig. 2: The Duke and Duchess of Connaught opening
Marine Drive on 5 August 1908.

heavy seas and rock falls deterred the tramway company from ever extending the network along here.

The line was laid and owned by Edmunson's Electricity Corporation, who also had tramway interests in Redruth, Cornwall, and Glossop in Derbyshire. Work began on 12 October 1903. By May the following year the system was installed, except for the Marine Drive section and the private road to the Spa. However, in total, only 2.97 miles of double track and 1.81 miles of single track were initially operated. The longest section of the double track was on Westborough, Falsgrave Road (Figure 3), and Foreshore Road. The system involved constructing tight curves at steep gradients. Between the seafront and the top of Vernon Road there was a difference of one hundred feet and a gradient of 1:10 on this section was the steepest on the entire network.

Fig. 3: Falsgrave Road,
showing the double track reducing to a single track

Over the roof of the *Aquarium* building below the Spa Bridge, built between 1874 and 1877, the rails had to be reinforced to take the weight of the tramcars (Figure 4). The entire system up to that point had cost £96,000 to construct.

Fig. 4: Laying the tramlines over the roof of the *Aquarium* in 1903. In the background is the Spa Bridge.

On 4 May 1904 there was a final inspection by officials of the Board of Trade, and at 3.30 in the afternoon of 6 May, passenger services commenced. The official opening of the system was a typically grand occasion with the Mayoress declaring the line open and the General Manager of the operating company, Mr. Edmunson, driving the first tramcar (Figure 5). By the time of the last tram that day, it was estimated that some 6000 passengers had used the tramway. The following day, ten thousand were carried and on 8 May, another 6000 passengers travelled on the system, which on Sundays ran services in the afternoon only, beginning at 2.30 pm.

Taylor's *Pictorial Guide to Scarborough* published soon after the tramway was opened, stated: *the new electric tramways which have just been put down through the principal streets will be found a great convenience to the public* – and so they were. For the next twenty-seven years, the Scarborough Tramways Company provided a public service throughout the town and

Fig. 5: The Mayoress opens the tramway system, 6 May 1904.

much of the surrounding area. The actual network that was operated was smaller than had been first authorised but was sound, and the basic route pattern was that of a figure-of-eight with three spurs. Over this system a variety of routes were worked.

Tram rails for the system were supplied by the North Eastern Steel Company, of Middlesbrough, each weighing 90 lb per yard. The track was laid to a gauge of 3 feet 6 inches.[1] Generally, the overhead lines were suspended from bracket-arm poles and span wiring, although centre poles were used along Foreshore Road. Electricity for the network was supplied from the Seamer Road Power Station by the Scarborough Electricity Supply Company.

The single track along Newborough and Westborough was controlled by coloured traffic light fitted to the tramway poles. The signals were activated by a mechanism on the overhead lines.

Track points were usually operated by the driver or conductor. However, at busy times, a 'points boy' switched points at the junction of Vernon Road and Westborough and Aberdeen Walk and Westborough.

When a car was ascending Vernon Road the driver would sound the gong on the tramcar alerting the 'points boy' to operate the mechanism. If no boy appeared, the driver would pick up a special bar and with a well-aimed swing from the cab, change the points himself.

The depot and workshops necessary for the maintenance of the tramcars was established on Scalby Road. At first there was a fleet of fifteen cars, which later increased to twenty-eight in total. Additional depot space on the site was constructed by a local contractor.

Fig. 6: Tramcar No. 22, built in 1905 and powered by a single 35 hp motor. This car could seat 20 passengers inside and 24 on the upper deck.

All the tramcars were conventional open toppers with three windows along the bottom deck and an open platform at each end (Figure 6). Because of the town's narrow streets the maximum width of each car could not exceed 6 feet 3 inches. On the upper deck, seats were arranged in two rows with twin seats on one side and a row of single seats on the other, separated by the gangway. On average each car could carry forty passengers seated, although a few bought in 1926 from Ipswich Corporation could seat 50 passengers.

All the tramcars had wooden bodies. The fleet livery was a deep maroon and cream. "Decency boards" (panels round the lower edge of the tram body to hide the bogies and running gear) were cream and along the rocker boards, the words 'Scarborough Tramways Company' appeared in capital letters. The bogies on to which the bodies were mounted were originally green but later re-painted red or black.[2]

From the outset seven routes operated around the town, but the number increased after the First World War. In 1906 a branch line along Sandside to the Old Pier was opened. There was also a link constructed to serve the Fish Quay, with the intention of carrying fish from the quay up to Falsgrave Railway Goods Station, however, this was never actually used. Following negotiations with the owners of the Spa, a track was eventually laid to that place.

For special events at the Spa, extra trams ran from all termini to the Spa, at a flat rate fare of 2*d*, increased to 3*d* after the end of the 1914-18 War.

'Specials' became a regular feature of tramway life. During Scar-borough's celebrated Cricket Festivals for instance, special cars ran from the depot to North Marine Road via the Railway Station and town centre.

Another special feature introduced in the year 1907 or 1908, was the 'Tour of the Tramways System', when, for six-pence the passengers could enjoy a 75-minute tour of all the tram routes and a walk with the driver through Alexandra Gardens to view North Bay. The route began at the Aquarium and ran along Foreshore Road, Eastborough, Newborough, Westborough, Falsgrave Road, Scalby Road, Prospect Road, Hoxton Road, Castle Road, North Marine Road, returning via Aberdeen Walk, Vernon Road and back to the Aquarium. On the circular routes, a '3*d* Special' was offered, and these became quite popular. Another short-lived novelty was the special car that took residents and visitors alike down to the Lifeboat Coffee House, on the seafront, for early morning coffee before breakfast.

Throughout its existence, the tramway has not been a success in the eyes of many. In October 1905, the company became involved in the first of a series of lawsuits that bedevilled the undertaking for much of its life. A tramcar reversed into a cab. Damages were subsequently awarded against the company and there was a great deal of adverse publicity. Yet for all that, the tramway system had an exemplary safety record.

The only major accident occurred many years later on 16 September 1925, when Car No. 21 was ascending Vernon Road from the seafront, lost traction and ran backwards down the incline, crashing through the roof of the Aquarium ballroom (Figure 7). Luckily there were no major casualties. The few passengers on board suffered only minor cuts and bruises and Driver Richardson, who stayed with the tramcar to the end, received only minor injuries and spent but a brief time in hospital.

The Scarborough tramway was introduced on a wave of optimism but folded up almost unnoticed. Ironically, almost from the beginning the company sowed the seeds of its own destruction. The relationship between the Tramways Company and Scarborough Corporation was apparently chequered, to say the least. Trouble arose when, in September 1910, the Company announced through the local press, without prior consultation, that after 15 October the winter service would cease – and immediately. Following that date, the services duly ended. The town, understandably was up in arms, as where the Corporation. They sent a delegation to the Board of Trade and after an enquiry; the Company was ordered to resume the service. The Company, in its defence, stated that in the previous year it had made a £2,000 loss in its operations principally through running a winter service.

Initially, after the hearing and judgement the Tramway Company took no action to provide a winter service as ordered and Scarborough Corporation was forced to take the matter further under the provisions of the Scarborough Tramways Act.

Fig. 7: Tramcar No. 21 in the ballroom of the *Aquarium*
after it had careered down Vernon Road out of control and plunged
through a wall on 16 September 1925. The tram was later rebuilt using a
former Ipswich Tramcar body.

Legal action was taken against the Company as a result of which they were fined ten shillings for each day when no service ran. Eventually the service was restored but, ironically, the Company found it cheaper to pay the fine rather than run an operation during the winter months.

This was just one in a catalogue of abrasive incidents between the Tramway Company and Scarborough Corporation, which undoubtedly contributed toward its eventual demise. Later, possibly poor management was responsible for the low monetary returns, and the Corporation, which was entitled to a profit share from the network, never received any money from the venture. The tramway system always appeared to be in a poor financial state. Because of this uneasy alliance between the Tramway Company and the Corporation, plus other factors, the system was always susceptible to attack from competitors.

In 1911 an offer to purchase the network was made by a company with a view to replacing the tramcars with trolley buses or motor buses. This proposal never matured, but illustrates the precarious position of the tramway system from an early period in its history.

Following World War I the system went into a steady decline. Motor transport really began to make its mark – it was so much more convenient and flexible than the tramway. To the critics the tramcar was slow, cumbersome and not very quiet or comfortable, and was now becoming an anachronism that was perceived as an obstacle to the progress of the evermore prolific motor car.

During the wartime years revenue on the tramway had fallen dramatically. After the war the Company's financial state was perilous. In order for the Scarborough tramway network to survive, the system was sold in January 1922 to a syndicate of London and Yorkshire businessmen trading as 'Seaton's Yellow Motor Buses'. The writing was on the wall for the tramcar.

The tramways manager, Mr. Moinet, remained in control, but the new proprietors introduced a bus service to run in conjunction with the tramway along Marine Drive and South Cliff. Unfortunately, however, Seaton's Yellow Motor Bus Company fared no better with tramway operations than their predecessor and by 29 May 1923, the Corporation were actively and openly engaged in obtaining a 'Tramway Abandonment Order'.

Scarborough Corporation had no wish to operate the system itself, and although the Order was turned down, negotiations were entered in to for winding up the system in June 1924.

Once again, a new local syndicate of businessmen saved the day. They bought out the network and proceeded to smarten up the operation, but to little avail.

In 1930 more negotiations were started for the abandonment of the system. The Corporation offered a purchase price of £19,500 for the track and ancillary equipment. In March of the following year, by 13 votes to 5, it was decided to compulsorily purchase the tramway from September 1931 under the terms of the Scarborough Corporation Act.

The Abandonment Bill necessary to wind up the system was deposited in Parliament and passed within weeks.

On 29 September 1931 the newly appointed Yorkshire Traffic Commissioners agreed to the tramway abandonment.

The next day, 30 September 1931 at 10.30 am the last tram, Car No. 12, one of the first of the fleet in operation, left the West Pier for the depot. There was little ceremony, the Company Manager, Mr. Cordukes was at the controls. Just after 11.15 pm Car No. 12 arrived back at the depot for the last time and Scarborough's tramways were no more.

It was reported that one or two of the passengers on the very last service had also ridden on the first, twenty-seven years earlier.

From start to finish the tramcars of Scarborough had carried over 45 million passengers and covered nearly six million miles.[3]

With the cessation of the tramway, the monopoly rights to carry passengers within the Borough boundary were given to

United Automobile Services – the largest local bus operator. However, they were not the only bus and coach operators in the district.

In the summer of 1906 the North Eastern Railway began a programme of motor charabanc tours from the Railway Station forecourt in Scarborough (Figures 8 & 9). Their vehicles, some on Leyland and others on Fiat chassis, proved extremely popular despite, the fact that they were open to the elements. Their routes took them up to the Moors or along the Forge Valley and provided a picturesque means of viewing the countryside, especially for visitors, and while they did not fill the primary requirements of a public transport system, they were effective in some measure in this.

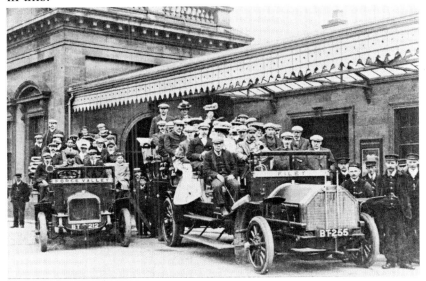

Fig. 8: Charabancs outside Scarborough Railway Station

After the end of the First World War and the discovery of the widespread benefits of motor transport, bus operators and services sprouted up throughout the land.

Fig. 9: A fully-laden charabanc leaving Scarborough Railway Station,
possibly *en route* to the Forge Valley.

In 1918, two Canadians, Messrs Abrams and Stevens started
running a local service from the market town of Pickering to
Scarborough using a four-seater motor car.

In 1921, the Speck Brothers pioneered a route from Scalby
to the town centre using a lorry fitted with rudimentary seating.
When not carrying passengers, the lorry carried firelighters man-
ufactured by the same company! Nevertheless, the service pros-
pered and Speck eventually sold out to the 'Peoples Motor
Services' of Balmoral Yard, Scarborough, which was started in
1922 with Messrs Gofton and Taylor as proprietors.

In that year another rival appeared on the profitable Scalby
route, Messrs Allen and Bootland. Their service terminated at the
Sun Inn, St Thomas Street, and the single fare from Scalby and
Cloughton to Scarborough was one shilling.

Allen's was one of the smaller bus companies that the
United Automobile Services bought out in 1928. From the mid to
late 1920s around the Scarborough district a few large bus companies plied for trade, and in particular the United Automobile

Services started operations thereabouts. Begun in 1912, they started operations in Suffolk and later in County Durham. The ambition of the founder, Mr. E B Hutchinson, was to provide a united and integrated service of buses and coaches over the entire eastern portion of England.

Through a policy of starting new routes, making agreements with other bus companies, or by simply buying out the opposition, this ambition was largely realised – and Scarborough became a part of it in 1923 when a small base was established in this popular Northern holiday resort – but not without fierce competition in the beginning.

In 1922 Alf Willings and Alwyn Noble began services from Hutton Buscel, Ayton and Scarborough and between Ebberston and Snainton to Scarborough. Forge Valley Motors, as it came to be known, proved a serious rival throughout its existence. Their slogan was: 'Travel Blue – Others Do!'

United never bought out this company, but in July 1961, through rationalisation it passed to them when they acquired the route from Scarborough to Hackness and Langdale End at a time when the company was run by Alwyn Noble alone after Mr. Alf Willings's retirement.

The Ebberston and Snainton route was also operated by Hardwick's Services, who had their company garage and depot at Snainton, built in 1936, and who became a subsidiary of Wallace Arnold Tours Limited. They plied the route from 1922 with a 14-seater bus.

Another company bought by United was Robinson's Motors in 1926, along with Abrams and Stevens. With the purchase of Robinson's and several other local bus operators, came the right to operate tours from the Railway Station forecourt.

This right had previously passed from the London & North Eastern Railway (successor to the NER) to Robinson's in 1923. This company operated a fleet of charabancs with 23 seats (Figure 10) which had a maximum speed of 23 mph.

Fig. 10: A fleet of Robinson's coaches in 1923, when they took over the services from LNER.

By acquiring the various bus services and operators the Scarborough district network of routes could be linked by United into the main network of North-East routes out of Whitby, and indeed, a through service from Scarborough to Middlesbrough could now be offered to the public. In 1928 the "Yorkshire Coast Express" started operating, and was, at that date, the only scheduled coach service that operated a timetable between Scarborough, Middlesbrough and the Tyneside towns and cities. The United Automobile Services, in establishing this route, pulled out all the stops to provide many comforts on the Express coaches. In the 1930s refreshments were available on board, with conductors in the unlikely guise of waiters when not collecting fares and issuing tickets! Buses were equipped with cigarette machines and, from 1932, many coaches were fitted with an observation deck in the manner of the American Greyhound coaches.

With the passing of the Railways Act in 1921, railway companies could buy shares in bus operators. This was in part a measure to try and control the inroads the motor bus was making

Fig. 11: A fully-laden charabanc on its way to Filey.

into the supremacy of the railway. In the Scarborough area, the LNER bought shares in the Peoples Motor Service, which was then renamed Scarborough District. Their principal routes ran from Scarborough to Cayton, Filey and Hunmanby (Figure 11). Later the Scarborough District Services was absorbed into United when the LNER, together with Tilling and British Automobile Tractions Limited, acquired a controlling interest in United Automobile in 1929.

On 2 November 1929, United bought out Bridlington & District, a company with its historical roots in charabanc tours which had begun in 1905. This gave United control of the Scarborough to Bridlington road and a depot was set up in Bridlington, which was also the base of the neighbouring East Yorkshire Motor Services.

United, in a matter of six or seven years, had now become the principal bus operator in Scarborough and the surrounding district.

In 1929 United opened a garage and depot at Vernon Road (Figure 12). A year later the district office moved from St Nicholas Street to Albemarle Crescent and a new bus station and office was built in Somerset Terrace, near the Valley Bridge, which remained in use until the late twentieth century.

Fig. 12: Drivers, fitters and staff of the United Automobile Services at their depot in Vernon Road, standing in front of a United bus showing route No. 3 - Railway Station - Dean Road - Corner Café.

Following United's appointment as the sole operator of the Scarborough Corporation services to replace the tramway, an agreement was entered into whereby United was to further develop routes within the borough boundary. This agreement necessitated United separating 'town' routes from 'out of town' or 'country' routes.

On country routes there were to be picking-up restrictions and a minimum fare within the borough boundary. Under a profit-sharing scheme the arrangement with United was that the Corporation would receive 1*d* per mile operated after the first 8*d* per mile earned. The Corporation would then take the next 3*d* per mile earned. Any remaining balances were shared equally between the two. To compensate for this, United for a number of years charged its passengers slightly higher fares on the Scarborough town services.

United took over the running of the town services from the tramways on 1 October 1931.

From 1931 onwards the 'Scarborough Town Agreement' between Scarborough Corporation and United stood until 1978 when it was scrapped (Figure 13). The monopoly was now broken and, with the end of the agreement, this not only eased the financial burden on the company but gave a better use of vehicles. A better choice of service for the passenger was offered as 'out of town' services could now pick up inside the old borough boundary. United could now also compete against the three major bus companies that had arrived in the district during the late 1960s and early 1970s – Scarborough United, West Yorkshire and the East Yorkshire – all of which at one time had their own bus stations in the town.

Today, of course, United itself no longer exists, being part of Arriva North-East, who in a complete circle, have acquired interests in railways and who operate throughout England and the Continent, running both public service routes and holiday coach tours.

With this creation of large global bus companies however, much of the joy and adventure of bus travel has ceased. Perhaps it is because of this that nowadays most buses look the same, and from this stems a deep nostalgia for the old buses and coaches of the 1920s and 1930s decades.

Fig. 13: Outside the Railway Station forecourt *c.* 1930, showing three types of public service vehicles - tramcar, charabanc and United motor bus - which were all in operation in this period.

Some of the many types of buses and trams that have been seen on the highways and byways of Scarborough.

Notes and References

1. Goode, C & Hamilton, Ross *Trams by the Sea.* Published on the 50th anniversary of the abandonment of Scarborough Tramways.
2. *ibid.*
3. *ibid.*

Chapter 4

Early Public Houses of Scarborough

All the comforts of life in a tavern are known,
'Tis his home who possesses not one of his own;
And to him who has rather too much of that one
'Tis the house of a friend where he's welcome to run;
The instant you enter my door you're my lord,
With whose tastes and pleasures I'm proud to accord;
And the louder you call and the longer you stay,
The more I am happy to serve and obey.

THE ABOVE INVITATION of 'mine host' might have been applicable in the period when these lines were written but, as the manners and customs of the people are apt to change with the times, we have no hesitation in saying there are thousands who hold a contrary opinion at the present day.

Having some recollection of a great number of public-houses which have vanished from our sight, we now reproduce a few of those which existed in 'Olden times', together with a number of incidents connected with them; and though the following may not embrace all the inns and taverns which at one time were to be found within the ancient borough of Scarborough, there will no doubt be sufficient to call to the mind of that venerable individual, the 'oldest inhabitant', reminiscences of days gone by and places of revelry in which he spent the heyday of his youth – or perhaps, in more mature years, amid the politicians of the period, settled the affairs of the nation, criticised the minister's speech, the progress of the war, or pledged eternal friendship in the social glass.

In the old town much business was done amongst the seafaring population and, to give a welcome to our jolly tars after a long voyage, there was a house near the harbour called the *Sailor's Return*, kept by Peggy Holland, and another of a similar character on Fowler's Hill, near the building stocks, kept by Betty Giles.

The *Spread Eagle*, in the same neighbourhood was for many years kept by Mr. Mark Tissiman and, as the shipyards were of full work and plenty of men employed, the *Shipwright's Arms* was opened for their accommodation by John Shaw and, more than forty years past, kept by William Lancaster.

Fig. 1: The *Lancaster Inn*, Sandside, was established by William Lancaster in 1875.

On the site of the entrance to the Gas Works, in Quay Street, stood an old-established house called the *Golden Ball*, kept by Robert Morwan, afterwards by his widow Nancy Morwan, and then by William Yates, who married into the family, and was there until the Gas Company purchased it.

This house was noted during the days of the Old Corporation for the prime old ale produced on St. Jerome's Day, the 30th September, when the election of bailiffs and other corporate business took place.

The *Town Hall* was where the Bethel now stands. In Quay Street also stood the White *Hart*, kept by John Oxley, a noted angler with rod and line; the Gas Company also removed this house.

The *Dog and Duck* was kept by William Burton, known as the 'York Butcher' and afterwards by his son.

A person named Setterington kept the *Ship Inn*, Sandside, in 1747.

William Salmon, Jeremiah Hudson, John Skelton, and others at one time kept the *Buoy Inn.*

In East Sandgate was a noted house kept by Jonathan Reed, and near St. Thomas's Church a blacksmith named Friars kept a house, and the *Crab and Lobster* was run by a person named Crawford.

The *Old King's Arms*, kept by James Hewitt and Thomas Mosey, was a house well frequented by sea captains.

The old *Long Room*, facing the Staith, was kept by George Chapman; the *Scarborough Volunteers* by Richard Laycock, tailor; the *Dolphin*, by Roger Crampton, who died in 1800; the *Three Tuns*, in Globe Street, by Betty Chatham, familiarly called 'Cheat 'em'.

The *Old Globe Inn* has had several proprietors in its time, and is one of the oldest established houses in the town. It was originally owned by Mr. William Stockdale, at which time Globe Street was called Stockdale Street.

This house was also kept by Mr. John Sedman, who died in 1778; by Mr. Richard Wilson, who died in 1796, in whose time the Freemason's Lodge was built, and by Mr. Richard Pearson, who died in 1797; by Mr. Peter Brown, who died in 1803; followed by Mr. Hammond, of the Local Militia, Mr. John Tissiman, Mr. John Chapman, and others.

It is stated that the stabling attached to the *Old Globe* was used for the accommodation of the first Royal Mail coach which came into Scarborough.

In St. Sepulchre Street was a house called the *Shepherd and Sheep*, kept by a person named Williamson.

The *Wheat Sheaf*, Cross Street, pulled down for the Market Hall, was kept by William Cross, who also worked as a coal porter.

The *Elephant and Castle* was also demolished as part of the Market Hall development. In 1796 it was kept by John Smelt; also by John Lawson, who, though possessed of but one arm, was acknowledged as one of the best billiard players of the day.

Francis Johnson, and others, also kept this house.

Close to the *Elephant* was the covered entrance to the old Shambles, above which stood the *Stag and Hounds*, which was reached by a flight of stairs from the street, and kept by Richard Garbutt.

A few doors below stood the *White Bear*, kept by Mr. Hutchinson, succeeded by John Leaf, who was there in 1804, then by George Reed and his widow.

Across the top of St. Sepulchre Street, from the old Shambles to Dumple, there stood a row of old-fashioned houses that were pulled down to make room for the Market Hall.

On one side of the Shambles, was a small shop formerly occupied by Mary Doughtry, a dealer in sweets, fruit and the like, and who sold smuggled gin. A Mrs. Scaling afterwards lived there.

On the other side of the archway was Betty Moffat's greengrocery shop, and close by was a narrow passage leading to some tenements behind the residence of Simon Spark, whitesmith, whose shop was in St. Sepulchre Street, where the Primitive Methodist Chapel now stands. He had the command of a field-piece in the Scarborough Volunteers which were raised from 1797 to 1807.

Adjoining his residence was a house formerly occupied by a family named Cass, and for many years after by Mr. Thomas Sedman, who kept the *Shoulder of Mutton*; but, after the old conduit was altered and a fountain placed there, the name of the house was changed to the *Fountain Inn*. After Miss Sedman retired it was taken by Mr. John Bell, head waiter from the *Crown*, who afterwards became proprietor of the *Queen's Hotel*.

The next house in the row above mentioned was formerly occupied by Mr. Robert Atkinson, ship owner, whose property it was, and afterwards by Mr. Rawson and others. Mr. Dent, leather-cutter, occupied the house before it was pulled down.

Adjoining it was the passage called Bennett's Entry, leading through into Cross Street.

Next to this passage was a small house in the corner, occupied by a person named 'Scotch Maggie', who struggled hard to bring up a family, having been deserted by her husband, Jack Leek (alias Lord Scarborough), who, when he 'retired' from sea-faring, became a notorious beggar.

At the corner of Carr Street stood the *Golden Last*, kept in former times by Nancy Weatherley, afterwards by Charles Owen, Edward Fowler, and Joseph Goodbarn, who died in 1804; his son, Joseph, who died in 1822, and then by his grandson, Joseph, and his great grandson, Joseph, whose widow resided there afterwards – her son's name also being Joseph.

The *Golden Last* has been rebuilt two or three times and enlarged since it was occupied by Edward Fowler.

Many years ago smuggling was extensively carried on in Scarborough and the surrounding neighbourhood, especially of Hollands gin, and it is related that during the time Charles Owen was at the *Golden Last* he had a large hogshead let into the floor of the kitchen hearth, which was covered over with a cinder grating, and in this receptacle he could stow away a number of small gin tubs when they were brought up from the shore.

So much money was made by these contraband transactions that he was wont to say that gold often came down the chimney to him.

In Merchant's Row, near Mr. Vassali's, was a quiet, respectable house called the *Steam Packet Inn*, kept by Mr. John Allen, and which was probably the first house in Scarborough which had a bagatelle table.

Further down, at the corner of Globe Street, was the *Mariners' Tavern*, kept by Mr. John Tissiman, William, his brother, and others; and, before it was pulled down for the East-borough improvement, by Mr. W. Dovey.

The Old Blue Bell, in Bland's-cliff, was at one time kept by Mr. Robert Marflitt, who died in 1791, and, during the smuggling times referred to, gin tubs were sent from here by post chaise at night.

Mrs. Marflitt continued to manage the house until her death in 1798. Afterwards, Mr. Harrison, Mr. Richard Hopper, and others, occupied *The Bell*, which was a great coaching house.

The Old Red Lion in Newborough was formerly kept by Mary Nicholson, Samuel Hardy, Mr. Lightfoot, and others. It was afterwards converted into an ironmongery establishment for Messrs. Simeon Lord & Co.

The George Inn has had a few changes. Among those who have occupied it we name Mr. Yeoman, Charles Owen, Miss Fox, Richard Towers, and others.

About the year 1760, *The New Inn*, Newborough, was kept by Mr. William Stephens, then by Jeremiah Hudson, James Harwood, and others.

The house and shop once occupied by Mr. William Wray, grocer, was formerly the *Granby Inn*, kept by Mr. John Southwell.

The *Grey Horse*, was kept by Mr. Thomas Walker. The *London Inn*, by Mr. Michael Clark, whose widow married Mr. Savery. For many years its business was conducted by Mr. Joseph Coates and then by his widow.

The Nag's Head (later the *Bar Hotel*) was kept by Mr. Jackson, and for a number of years by Mr. Robert Miller, his widow and their family after them.

The *Pied Bull*, Without-the-Bar, was occupied by Mr. William Croasdale in 1793; he died in 1797, and was succeeded by his nephew, Mr. John Houson, who died in 1840. Mrs. Reed and others followed. In connection with this house there was

probably one of the most extensive of stable yards in the king-
dom, with a large pond in the centre. Later the *Pied Bull* became
the *Bull Hotel*.

On 21st May in 1733 the following advertisement appeared in the *York Chronicle*:

> 'William Croasdale and Jane his wife, late of the *Spread
> Eagle*, Boroughbridge, have removed to the genteel and
> commodious *Py'd Bull Inn*, without the Gates, in Scarbor-
> ough, and furnished the same in a very genteel manner;
> they return their most grateful thanks to the gentlemen,
> ladies and others for their past favours at Boroughbridge,
> and hope for a continuance of the same at this place. All
> noblemen, gentlemen, ladies and others who please to
> honour them with their commands, may depend on good
> accommodation, and civil usage, by their most obedient
> and humble servants, – William and Jane Croasdale. *NB* –
> Genteel post-chaises and good horses, with careful drivers,
> will be ready on the shortest notice.'

The *Beverley Arms*, Newborough, belonged to James Donkin,
Billy Donkin's father; also kept by Mr. Monkman, barber, Mr.
Duck, and others.

In Long Room Street stood the *Black Swan*, formerly kept
by Robert Beal. The *Old Long Room* (from which the street was
renamed) was kept by Mr. Edward Donner, who died at Scalby in
1800. Here assemblies were held every Monday, Wednesday, and
Friday, during the season. It was afterwards called *Donner's
Hotel*, now the *Royal*.

The *Old Assembly Rooms* were conducted by Mr. William
Newstead, who had assemblies every Tuesday, Thursday, and
Saturday, during the season. In the year 1800 this building was
converted into the *Town Hall*, and although it was rebuilt in 1871,
it still retains the name of the *Old Town Hall*.

In the same street was the *Hand of Providence*, kept by
Charles Waud; the *Hole-in-the-Wall*, by Nancy Duggleby; the
Mariner's, by Elizabeth Westlake.

The Plough Inn, Tanner Street, was a much larger house than at present, with stabling behind. In 1795 *The Plough* was kept by Mr. Samuel Jordan, and afterwards by George Wright, David Nicholson, George Coulgon, William Newton, and others.

In the same street was the *Ship*, kept by Fanny Carling.

In Queen Street was the *Blacksmith's Arms*, kept by Mr. Frank Temple and Mr. John Ruddock, pulled down to make way for the Wesleyan Chapel, and nearly opposite was the *Bay Horse*, kept by Edward Liddle, Wellburn Bland, Godfrey Womersley, who afterwards kept the *Golden Lion* in the same street.

The Grapes was kept by Mr. Thomas Dunwell, and the *Talbot*, by Mr. Theophilus Rivis, Mr. Hutchinson, Mr. Jonas Hammond, &c.

In Bird Garth was the *Bell*, kept by Nancy Firth.

The *Cross Keys* kept by John Thornhill, was a favourite house with the Vicar of Scarborough, and it became a common saying, "If you want a glass of good ale, follow Parson Hewitson and his clerk, Huntriss, to John Thornhill's."

Martha Duncanson had a tavern in Long Westgate, and near to Long Greece Steps was a house called the *Tartar Frigate*. Barbary Starr kept a tavern in Castlegate.

Martha Hawson had the *Hand and Sceptre*; Betty Coultas, the *Sunderland* Bridge; Mr. Owen and Mr. Siddall, the *King's Arms*, in King Street; Mr. Robert Powley, the *Cabbage*, now the *Star*, which was afterwards kept by Mr. William Cross, and his widow, who married Mr. George Barker.

Near Aberdeen Walk Corner was a snug, cosy house, called the *Spaw Inn*, kept by Mr. Francis Shaw; also *the Ship*, in Church Street, by Mr. Thomas Thornton.

The *Ship*, at Peasholm, kept by Mr. Sandwith, was a noted place for holiday parties, and at Easter for rolling eggs. A very amusing event took place here, which shows what pranks were played in those days.

"Mr. Thomas Walshaw, always ripe for fun, and a companion, Mr. George Tomlinson, for a spree assumed the garb of fortunetellers, which they for some time practised without detection. On market days they visited the Plough, *other days the* Ship. *They had many visitors and great fame, as they knew most of the people who came to them, and therefore had no difficulty in telling their past and present events. By this freak they realized a good sum, and then invited all who had patronized them to a splendid supper, after which they made known to the guests who they really were, and had a merry termination."*

The following account of the customs and amusements of the visitors at this long-established watering-place in the year 1733 may prove interesting, relating as it does to the early public houses or 'ordinaries' of Scarborough.

"The town is populous (containing, by computation, about 2,000 families) and well built; the houses, for the most part, uniform, neat, and commodious. The streets are most of them very spacious, so that coaches may pass and re-pass without any difficulty or inconvenience. The lodgings here are very reasonable, and well furnished, there being here an upholsterer from London. A shower of rain puts no stop to the diversions of the place, for you have chairs from London, which ply in the principal parts of the town.

"The High Street is called the Newborough, out of which runs another up to the Long Room, *which stands towards the end of the town, on the top of a cliff, from whence, by a gradual descent, you go down to the Spaw. This is a noble spacious building, sixty-two feet long, thirty feet wide, and sixteen*

high; the situation being so lofty, commands a prospect over the sea and you may sit in the windows and see the ships sailing at several leagues distance. Here are balls every evening, when the room is illuminated like to a Court assembly (and indeed, for the great number of noble personages present, it may very justly be called so). Gentlemen (only) pay for dancing one shilling each. On one side of the room is a music gallery, and at the lower end are kept a Pharo bank, a hazard table, and fair chance; and in the side rooms, tables for such of the company as are inclined to play at cards. Below stairs you have billiard tables: it is kept by Mr. Vipont, master of the Long Room *at Hampstead.*

"There is no ordinary here, but gentlemen may have anything dressed in the most elegant manner, the house being provided with cooks from London. Everything is conducted in the politest manner by Vipont, who is a perfect master of his business. Gentlemen and ladies subscribe here likewise five shillings. There are several ordinaries in the town, the principal of which are the New Inn, *the* New Globe, *the* Blacksmith's Arms, *the* Crown and Sceptre, *and the* Old Globe.

"The company dine commonly about two, and have ten or a dozen dishes, one of which is generally rabbits, which you have here in the utmost perfection; their mutton is, I think, at least equal to Banstead Downs, and the nearness of this town to the sea supplies them with plenty of the finest fish at very reasonable rates; and for poultry, they have here a poulterer who finds it worth his while coming from London every summer. It is usual to drink a glass of Spaw water mixed with your wine at dinner.

"Persons of all ranks, gentlemen and ladies together, sit down without distinction, each paying their club, which is one shilling; after which, they collect round the company for wine, etc. (called the extra-ordinary), which is generally about one shilling more. This last formerly used to be paid by the Gentlemen only; but that complaisant custom is now laid aside, and the ladies are brought in to pay an equal share of the whole reckoning. This method of ordinaries is vastly commodious for strangers, and affords an opportunity of being acquainted with the company. In the afternoon are plays acted, to which most of the gentry in the town resort. After the play is over, it is customary to go to the Long Room *again, where they dance or play till about nine, and then sup in company again."*

Finally, having started with a verse, I shall conclude with another.

The Beehive Inn, on Sandside, lost its licence in 1904 after complaints by the clergy because of the noise and drunkenness. A sign above the door read,

Within this hive we are all alive,
good ale will make you funny,
if you are dry as you pass by,
step in and taste our honey'.

Fig. 2: The remains of the *Strawberry Garden Inn*, *c.* 1880,
which probably did a roaring trade quenching thirsts
during the fruit picking season.

Fig. 3: Scalby Mills Hotel.

Chapter 5

Scarborough Castle: a Brief History

S CARBOROUGH CASTLE is set dramatically on top of a headland rising three hundred feet out of the North Sea. This formidable site was first occupied in the Iron Age. Later the Romans built a signal station on the cliff edge to give early warning of pirate raids.

Fig. 1: Scarborough Castle from Oliver's Mount.

The medieval castle appears to have been begun before 1135 by William le Gros, Earl of Albemarle. The chronicler, William of

Newburgh, states that the Earl constructed a curtain wall and tower.[1]

When the castle came into Crown control in 1154 on the accession of Henry II, the same tower is described as having fallen into decay, which may explain why the monarch ordered the construction of the surviving keep.

The Pipe Rolls record expenditure on the castle amounting to more than the keep.

In addition to the keep there are several structures that date from the second half of the twelfth century and which could have been erected at this time. These include much of the curtain wall of the inner bailey and two associated gatehouses.

King John spent considerable sums on Scarborough Castle amounting to more than £2,291.[3] Unfortunately, records do not specify how this money was spent. Architecturally, the substantial building known as Mosdale Hall and much of the curtain wall and towers appear to date from this period.

During Henry II's reign resources were committed to much repair work within the castle and to the construction of the 'Great Gate'. However, a survey on the state of the fortress in 1260 suggests that the buildings had fallen into a poor state of repair. The roofs of the great hall, great chamber, kitchen and tresconce reported to be uncovered in several places and repairs were required to the floors, windows and doors of the keep. Most of the main defences of the castle were also described as in need of urgent attention.

Overseers were appointed in June 1260 to see that repairs were put in hand 'against the coming winter'.[4]

If work was indeed done, it seems to have been ineffective and by 1278 it was estimated that £2,200 was needed to put things right.

By 1312 the castle was in a sufficiently good state to withstand a siege when Edward II's favourite, Piers Gaveston, took refuge in the castle; only the lack of provisions forced his surrender.[5]

Repairs to the stronghold were ordered in 1313, which included the addition of a porch to the queen's chamber.[6] This can perhaps be identified with the porch at the north-eastern end of Mosdale Hall, which (unlike the porch at the opposite end) is a later addition.

Throughout the remainder of the fourteenth century the castle appears to have continued to deteriorate, with occasional sums of money allocated to arrest some of the worst dilapidations.

The stimulus of the threatened French invasions of the late fourteenth century led to a survey of the repairs required at the castle in 1393.

*The 13th century seal of the
Borough of Scarborough*

A programme of works was begun by the constable, John de Mosdale, between 1396 and 1400. This included the construction of a new hall which has been identified by means of the survey of 1538 as the structure in the outer ward built against the curtain wall.[7] However, it seems more likely that this work related to the reconstruction of the thirteenth-century hall which stood to the north; this building shows evidence of extensive work during the fourteenth century.

The castle was granted to Richard, Duke of Gloucester, but returned to Crown control after Richard's rise to power.

The castle was besieged twice in the sixteenth century: during the Pilgrimage of Grace in 1536 and the rising of Thomas Stafford in 1557.

On the first occasion the castle sustained some damage, which was subsequently repaired.

In 1619 the castle was granted to John, Earl of Holderness by James I and, after the Earl's death, to Francis Humbleton.

During the Civil War it was initially held by Sir Hugh Cholmley, of Whitby, for Parliament – until March 1643 when he changed sides to the Royalist cause! However, the garrison seized the castle for Cromwell until Captain Browne Bushell, nephew of Cholmley, regained it for the Royalists.

He himself, later changed sides, and was subsequently executed on Tower Hill as a traitor following the Civil War.

The castle was eventually besieged by Parliamentary forces in January 1645. A gun called the 'Cannon Royal' was mounted in St. Mary's church to bombard the castle. This piece of artillery was responsible for much of the present destruction of the keep.

Eventually, in July 1645, the castle fell and Parliament allocated £5,000 for its repair.

A further siege took place between September and December 1648, with the castle held for the King. The damage after this second siege appears to have been sufficiently extensive that the order for the castle's demolition in July 1649 was not carried out.

The stronghold was subsequently used as a prison and barracks, the latter being built during 1746 after the Jacobite Rebellion of the previous year.

The last action the castle saw was in December 1914 when the German fleet shelled both the castle and the town.

The castle headland is roughly triangular, with precipitous drops to the sea on the east and north-west.

On the south-west there is merely a wide, deep ravine separating the castle from the town. It was along this side that William le Gros erected his curtain. Initially there was no keep, but a gate tower probably stood on the site of the present entrance. Consequently, Scarborough gives the appearance of being modelled on Richmond Castle in its original form.

The Main Gateway or 'Great Gate', Scarborough Castle.

At first no flanking towers existed. The semi-circular projecting bastions date from King John's reign. Eight survive and a ninth has perished, but they cannot account for all of the £2,000 or so that he spent on the castle. Admittedly he also built Mosdale Hall, which is now faced in 18th century brick.

Only a narrow causeway at the west angle connects the castle headland to the town, which was sacked by the Scots in 1318, but the castle was left untouched.

On the townward side stands the barbican, a small inclosure with a round-towered outer gatehouse. It was added by Edward III as a precaution against French raids during the Hundred Years War, and forms the most recent part of the castle's defences.

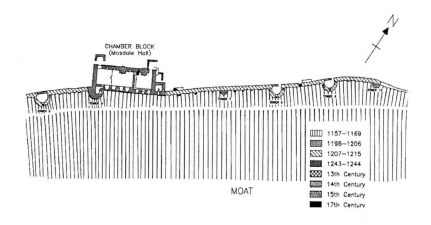

Scarborough Castle: Plan of outer Ward and Curtain.

The narrowest part of the causeway was closed by the thirteenth-century gate tower, now reduced to its base. There are deep chasms to front and rear, originally crossed by drawbridges (and now spanned by stone bridges). After that comes the steep ascent to the keep.

Henry II's keep is the dominant feature of the castle. Unlike the one in Richmond, the keep here is not a conversion of

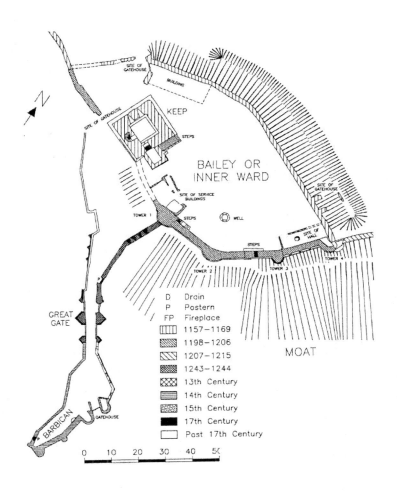

Scarborough Castle:
Plan of the inner Ward and
Barbican.

the original gatehouse but it is placed in a commanding position overlooking the castle entrance. This tall, square tower was a little larger than Richmond's keep. It is not easy to compare, however, because of the destruction during the Civil War. A flight of steps leads to the first-floor entrance, but the protective fore-building has been reduced to its footings.

Though generously provided with windows, the upper floors do not have the profusion of mural chambers that characterise the later keeps of Henry II. A ruined curtain around the keep creates a small inner bailey.

The surviving elements of the enclosing curtain wall of the inner bailey are from two phases of construction. The earlier is indicated by the footings of a rectangular gatehouse, with associated drawbridge spanning the inner ditch, on the eastern side of the bailey. Evidence of a second gatehouse of the same period further north is represented by one surviving jamb. Between these two entrances a stretch of curtain running north to south is also of this work. A row of evenly spaced joist holes is evidence for an early building on the northern-most stretch of this wall (adjacent to the position of the gatehouse into the third ward).

This work, along with the keep, is what survives of Henry II's expenditure on the castle between the years 1157-1169.

The second phase of work was the rebuilding of the south-west curtain wall, forming part of King John's development of the castle.

Near Mosdale Hall are the foundations of William le Gros' original hall.

Further east on the cliff edge some fragments of the medieval chapel over lie the Roman signal station. This was probably destroyed in 1066 when the town of Scarborough was burned by Hardrada and Tostig before their defeat by King Harold at Stamford Bridge. The nearby well is the Holy Well of Our Lady on Roman foundations.

The keep of Scarborough Castle.

Notes and References:

1. VCH Yorkshire, North Riding, ii.
2. Brown, R A, Colvin, H M & Taylor, A J *The History of the King's Works*, ii.
3. Brown, R A 'Royal Castle-building in England 1154-1216', English Historical Review, vol. 70, pp351-98.
4. *Cal. Liberate Rolls* 1251-60, pp 512-13.
5. Gaveston was taken to Warwick were he was executed.
6. *Cal. Patent Rolls, 130-13, p 466.*
7. Port, G. *Scarborough Castle*. 1989.

Chapter 6

Recollections of Rowntree's

THE COMPANY OF WILLIAM ROWNTREE AND SONS of Westborough was originally founded by Mr. Robert Clemesha in the year 1781, and after numerous changes in the constitution of the business, Mr. William Rowntree, who in 1845 had been in business with a Mr. Stickney, and was related through

Fig. 1: Nineteenth century public notice displaying the names of Stickney and Rowntree as subscribers

marriage, became sole proprietor (Figure 1). During succeeding years Rowntrees steadily developed various other branches associated with the drapery trade from what had been essentially a company noted for the manufacture of hats. From comparatively small beginnings, the house grew into a company with hardly a rival in the North of England, and was second only to one or two stores in London for reputation.

Fig. 2: The village store of Wallis & Blakeley in Scalby, later taken over by William Rowntree & Son.

Initially the different departments were scattered about the town of Scarborough and, indeed, they had branches throughout the district, where Rowntrees adopted a policy of buying out other small village stores, such as that of Wallis and Blakeley, in Scalby (Figure 2). However, by the mid nineteenth century they had become so huge in Scarborough, that new premises were required and, subsequently, on Thursday 21 September 1882, a vast emporium was opened in Westborough, stretching from number 33 to number 39 (Figure 3).

Fig. 3:
Rowntree's new department store, opened in 1882. Situated at the corner of Westborough and York Place.

It was announced that the business here was to be managed by Mr. William Stickney Rowntree, James Henry Rowntree and Allan Rowntree, the original Mr. William Rowntree, senior, having retired from the business some years prior to 1882.

A trade journal published soon after the new Westborough store had opened, described the building as:

'. . . *a fine example of the French Renaissance period, and the entire façade is carried out in white Barnard Castle stone. The splendid windows, forming ten distinct bays, have frontages to the main thoroughfare and to York Place at the junction of which streets the block is located . . .The edifice rises to an elevation of four storeys and the green Welsh slates with which the whole is crowned lend a very pleasing effect to the tout ensemble. We need hardly say that the attractiveness of the exterior finds its corresponding counterpart in the completeness of the interior.*

*Elegance, commodiousness and perfect taste are
the keynotes of every department . . .'* (Figure 4)

Fig. 4: A glimpse
of the Furnishings
Department in the
newly opened store

From the beginning to its end, the family run business of Rowntrees, founded by members of the famous Quaker family of York,
saw large numbers of staff pass through its stores both in Scarborough and York.

Many have died, passed without trace, but a few, who still
meet regularly, have taken time to jot down recollections of life
in this famous department store.

JEAN WALLINGTON'S earliest recollection of Rowntrees store in
Scarborough was of being taken there in the 1930s when her mother
bought a white shantung blouse for her school days.[1]

Her account follows:

Whenever I wore that blouse I felt great in it . . . it had
quality and style, which were the hallmark of Rowntrees. She also
bought a cocktail set – six glasses and a decanter – for a rich aunt
who lived in Bournemouth, which she chose from the China
Department; a suitable gift for someone who had everything.

In 1947, when my future husband was on leave from the
Parachute Regiment, we went to Rowntrees every morning to the
Orange Room for coffee and toasted teacakes. His last night
coincided with a dance at the *Royal Hotel* for Rowntrees' em-

ployees and friends; we had a marvellous time and little did I realise that eight years later I would be part of that happy gang.

In May 1955, I answered an advert in the newspaper for a shorthand typist in the Correspondence Room of Rowntrees. In my letter I asked if they had any part-time vacancies, as I only wanted to work from 9.30 am until 3.30 pm in order to be able to take my two children to and from school.

By a strange coincidence, a Mrs. Doris Spaven had also written in answer to the advertisement asking for afternoon work, and we were jointly given the job on a month's trial.

We stayed for sixteen years.

Fig. 5:
The Correspondence
Room in 1963.

The Correspondence Room (Figure 5) was up a hidden staircase at the side of the Bedding Department. Mrs. Jane Binks was the Supervisor, and Mrs. Elsie Howes and Miss Beryl Thompson, were the two senior typists, with Misses Lupton, Matson and Wild, and Doris and I making up the staff of eight.

In our world the day began with the menu for the Restaurant being typed onto a stencil and duplicated. Throughout the remainder of the hours junior members of the staff would bring up hand-written letters from different Departments and place them in a box on a table at the head of our stairs. We then took them out, typed them up, had them checked by Mrs. Binks, and then placed them in a pigeon-hole to go back down to the Department later in the day. Of course, everyone picked out the ones which were easiest to read, and I usually ended up with Miss

Smithie's letters which were rather indecipherable as her assistant, to whom she dictated had arthritis in her hands. We also duplicated store notices, prepared estimates for decoration work and bills for funerals.

Miss C Ganderton was Complaints Secretary in those early days. Any complaint coming into the store had to be typed out in triplicate, and she had to deal with the complaint the same day. Rowntrees believed that a dissatisfied customer spread dissatisfaction far and wide and felt this should be nipped in the bud.

At the beginning of my employment, each Department had a Buyer and a Department Manager. The Buyer went off to exotic places buying on behalf of the store, whilst the Department manager saw to the everyday running of the Department. In time these two positions were merged into one.

One of my earliest experiences in my first week was to go to Mr. Eric Mason for dictation; a piece for the local newspaper, which included the word 'boutique' which completely stumped me when transcribing in shorthand. Fortunately Mrs. Binks helped me out over the word, but I had completely lost touch with fashion being at home for eight years since marriage.

Gradually, through the march of progress, it became quicker for anyone with a lot of letters to use a dictaphone. Mr. A J Wallis,[2] used to bring up a tape of correspondence to be done 'yesterday' by one of the 'minions'. These letters were invariably to people with outstanding accounts and now and again, strangely, to people who had paid twice!

We always had to look busy, which normally we were, but if we had a spare moment we put a label in the typewriter to look busy in case a Director walked through.

Eventually my job mostly involved assisting Miss Lillian Newton, the Customers' Adviser, who received letters from all over the world requesting goods to be sent, or asking for presents to be bought and delivered to relatives and friends. Christmas was especially exciting in this department as Miss Newton would be asked to choose so many presents, have them gift-wrapped and then dispatched to delighted recipients.

Easter Saturday was said to be the busiest day of the year and most clerical staff had to help out on that day in the Departments, as sales assistants. My first experience of this was in the Blouse Department, where Miss M Lishman told me never to say 'Can I help you?' For if the customer said 'no', then you were stuck, whereas, if I said, 'Isn't this lovely material?' one immediately gained the customers attention and could possibly lead on to sell the garment. My first lesson in the art of selling!

June was an exciting time because of Scarborough Festival Week and the Parade, which took place on the Wednesday afternoon. Mr. Mason would organise the 'Store Float' with the help of the Display Department, and what they jointly produced, was always judged the best in the show. Staff would be allowed to go and stand on the tiny balcony outside Mr. Scott's office in the Linen Department and throw balloons down as our Float passed underneath. Such fun!

July and August were busy months, with Rowntrees packed with shoppers. Invariably weekly visitors arrived in Scarborough on the Saturday, spent Sunday on the beach, and on Monday came to look round the shops. One thing I remember is how many Mondays were wet, and shoppers with umbrellas and plastic raincoats dripped all over the store. It was terrible to have to go through a crowded department – one always ended up as wet as them!

By September Rowntrees was preparing for Christmas, advertising a catalogue and dealing with enquiries that came in to the Customers' Adviser. By the start of December our Display Department had put up all the gorgeous trimmings throughout the ground floor departments, each year a different theme, and Father Christmas would already have arrived in his Grotto for the Christmas period.

Rowntrees of Scarborough featured some of the most inviting and glorious Christmas Grottoes in the area. Father

Christmas (Figure 6) in attendance so bright, merry and jovial; his gloves white, never soiled or grubby grey; his make-up perfection, and not a wrist-watch to be seen! His black boots edged with white fur, and polished every day so that you could see your face in them. Dear Arthur Belt was the favourite Father Christmas of all time, so professional – and how both the children and adults loved him.

Fig. 6: Father Christmas and Arthur Belt,
enjoying a chat in the staff restaurant.

Each and every year Arthur would arrive at the store weeks in advance of the Christmas season to have his costume properly fitted. He would laugh and say, 'I must have it right, and this year I think I have put on a few inches!' and his eyes would twinkle. The white gloves were always renewed, a pair for wearing, a pair in the wash and a pair in reserve.

In those days the people entered Rowntrees through the main door in Westborough with the Cosmetics Department to the left, Millinery to the right, Ladies Hosiery straight ahead, down the centre to Handbag's, with the Man's Shop to the far left, Shoes near left and then on to Coats and Dresses. At the far end the stairs went down to Lingerie and Children's Wear. Up the main staircase for Carpets, Hardware, China, Soft Furnishings and Linens. Up again for Furniture and Toys, the 'Decoration Centre' and finally the Restaurant. On this floor too, was the Staff Office presided over by Miss M Calvert, a very charming and kindly person, with her staff: Elsie and Barbara.

Up here also, in the 1950s, was the library, ably run by Mrs. Patterson and her assistant, a very quiet young lady named Miss Ann Early. The library closed soon after I joined Rowntrees. In later years, Miss Early was often to be seen around the town in a red Spanish gown with a red rose in her hair, sometimes dancing in the precinct.

When Mr. A. Smithies left the restaurant a Mr. Brian Hill took over and soon after this a Food Department was opened on the ground floor where the Man's Shop had been. Afterwards, a Mr. John Topham took over as manager. This Department almost equalled Fortnum and Masons – it stocked so many varieties of food not found anywhere else 'up North'. When Mr. Topham left, after Debenhams had taken over and closed the Food Department, he started his own very successful business in Somerset Terrace.

In a building behind the store, parallel with Brunswick Terrace, the Counting House staff dealt with all the accounting side of the business. Mrs. Peggy Walker was in charge of this. Whenever we went to her for dictation, we had to pass through a small office opposite the Hardware Department and over the 'cat-walk' into the Counting House. This was a rather perilous journey over duckboards suspended above a glass roof to our left, and we were fearful lest we slip! We had to make another eerie journey to seek out a Buyer in her office behind the showrooms, which was behind the windows in York Place.

This was a warren of tiny passages that should have been in York Castle Museum. Little did the visitors to the store realise that behind the beauty of the shop-front were such Dickensian areas.

Fig. 7: Staff at the *Royal Hotel*, 24 January 1967. (Men, l - r) Eric Mason, Edward W. Neighbour, Eric Archer. (Ladies, l - r) Miss N. L. Smith and Jean Wallington.

Each year a party for the staff was organised by the Staff Council (Figure 7). Usually this was held at the *Grand* or *St Nicholas Hotel*.

One year, we had a party in our own restaurant organised by Mr. Eric Mason who made a gorgeous fresh fruit salad. I was roped in to help with the washing up afterwards and couldn't believe my eyes when I saw the wooden troughs and soda used to wash the pots. I never realised the restaurant staff had to use such archaic methods.

Juniors came and went in the Correspondence Room; they seemed to stay about two years and then moved on to better jobs in the town. Rowntrees prided themselves on the good grounding these girls received from Mrs. Binks. Mary Matson, then Brenda Wild, Elsie Arnell, Margaret Milburn, Pat Kidd, Miss Oliver, Doris Chapman, Sue Appleton, June Williams, Margaret Banks, Marilyn Williams, Kate Hepworth, Gail Manging – what a jolly crowd they were over the years.

In October 1957, the Asian 'Flu virus hit Scarborough and, of course, Rowntrees. Three of us, Mary Matson, Betty Maclaren and I were the only three unaffected among the office staff and we did the work of eight in the Correspondence Room while the 'flu raged and ran its course. Chaotic, but fun!

In November of the following year, Miss Lillian Newton retired after thirty-four years as Customers' Adviser. She was followed by Miss McClair, and then Mrs. E Flack, who both worked under the same name of 'Miss Newton' in order to keep customer continuity. In 1968 I was offered the position of Customers' Adviser until Debenhams discontinued the service (Figure 8). These were three of my happiest working years – the variety of tasks was tremendous.

Fig. 8: Mr. Eric Mason and 'Miss Newton' Jean Wallington present a prize to the winner of the Frigidaire Competition.

In May 1960, as a service to customers, the store provided television sets in various parts of the building for shoppers to watch the wedding of Princess Margaret. It was surprising how many staff 'went walkabout' through the store that day to get a glimpse of the celebrations.

When Miss Barker, the Director's Personal Secretary retired, Mary Matson did her work until Miss Naylor-Gaunt was appointed. Miss Gaunt had served time in the WRNS during

Fig. 9: The wedding day of HRH Princess Margaret and Anthony Armstrong Jones, 6 May 1960.

World War II, and later worked as a journalist. She did shorthand in a manner that was strange to see and she brought a breath of excitement to the clerical side.

In 1963 Mrs. Howes left to work at St Mary's Hospital and then Mrs. Binks retired. Miss Matson was promoted to Correspondence Room Supervisor until she herself left when expecting her first child. I then became Supervisor until I was promoted to Customers' Advisor. As Mrs. Howes had also been Advisory Secretary when she left, I was asked to take over this work too, which entailed being secretary to four executives who met monthly. This was very interesting work and every January I was taken out by them for a dinner as a 'thank you'. These were delightful meals – some at the *Royal Hotel*, sometimes at the *Pavilion* and once at the *Viking Hotel* in York.

Mr. Mason always supervised the menus which were superb and on each occasion a little gift was left on my plate – Chinese hankies, a fan, a Minton dish and so on – all happy reminders of those wonderful days.

For several years I was also Editor of the Rowntree *Staff Journal*, a magazine which came out quarterly. I was assisted in this venture by Mr. Robin Horspool. Although the idea was for staff to contribute articles, Robin and I invariably wrote most of the magazine's contents.

In December 1965 Debenhams took over Rowntrees, but for the first five years there was little change. However, by 1970 differences began to be apparent, Departments had to improve on their previous yearly figures and greater profits had to be made.

No longer was service to the customer the number one priority.

The Customers' Advisors post was axed.

In early 1971 the new decimal currency was introduced and a promotion was staged to help the shopper get used to 'Decimalisation' (Figure 10). This was the last customer event I was involved in. In August that year I resigned from the store with great sadness.

Fig. 10: 'Decimalisation Day', 15 February 1971. The Rowntree Store Information Bureau staffed by (l - r seated) Jean Wallington, Miss Dodds and Miss Mullen.

*   *   *   *   *

ATHOL J. WALLIS left Ackworth School in July 1936 with little idea of what he would like to do and no particular qualifications other than a love of natural history. It was soon quite clear, however, that to find any paid employment in that field of work with the minimum of qualifications was quite impossible.

He writes:

I first went to the Leeds University Library in response to an advertisement, but was not selected, nor did the Rowntree Cocoa Works in York consider me suitable for employment in their office. As my family were Quakers, we were already known to all the Directors of W. Rowntree & Sons Limited and, in fact, the Secretary at that time, Mr. Stevenson, was by marriage an uncle of mine. So mother went down to see him at the shop to ask if he could give me an apprenticeship in the Counting House. This was in September and his response was, 'Yes, but not until December'. 'This is too long to have this youth hanging round my neck; can't he come and work for you until December for nothing?' And for three months I was an extra member of staff with no specific duties, quite unpaid!

At that time the Counting House Manager was Mr. William Poole, and he had no specific work that he could give me so I was given all manner of jobs to do. This meant that when my apprenticeship began, I already knew much about the Counting House, which held me in good stead as the years went by.

One of the people I worked with during that early period was Cecilia Meade, who all the younger members of staff regarded as something of a dragon, but who is now one of the Rowntrees' Pensioners who I have the pleasure of looking after.

One recollection I have of that period, is that in those days small purchases made from local business people, mainly consisting of food for the Restaurant, was paid out of petty cash. Every so often I was given a number of bills and the money needed to pay them and sent round the town to pay the various shopkeepers. This nearly always meant that I came home with the odd sixpence in my pocket, handed back to me as a gratuity by one of the shopkeepers.

Having no real qualifications for progressing upwards within the business, I began a Correspondence Course to qualify as a Chartered Secretary. This meant long periods of study after a day's work at the office, and I took the first of two examinations needed just after the outbreak of World War II. This interrupted the rest of my studies, and I had to spend six years away from the store working in the Friends' Ambulance Unit. Here I served unpaid, but it was a period during which I met Hannah who became my wife in 1946 when I returned home and once again took up my employment at the store.

The first part of the Counting House that I returned to, was the Wages Office. At that time Rowntrees was employing somewhere in the region of 600 staff, and I believe I got to know everyone and could put a face to every name on every pay packet.

In those days all staff were paid weekly in cash. Mr. James Rowntree, who had a Swiss wife named Esther, liked to hand out the pay packets himself. He, however, had an unfortunate habit, and was followed round by Phyllis King, who would take the pay packets back and give them to the right people!

From the Wages Office I gradually progressed through the ranks, attaining eventually the position of Counting House Manager. Two members of staff I remember from those times were Frank Devonshire and Mr. Greenlay. These two were confirmed bachelors and spent much of their spare time together. I know that on two evenings each week they went to the cinema together. On Wednesday evenings they chose a film they particularly wished to see at one of the five cinemas in town, but on Saturday they went to the Capitol Cinema no matter what film was on show.

I next succeeded to the position of Assistant Secretary after Margaret Nevitt, who was quite convinced at the time that I was incapable of performing the duties required. Ultimately, however, I proved her wrong and moved on to become Administrative Director and Secretary of the Company, having by then, passed my final examination as an Associate of the Chartered Institute of Secretaries. In 1960 I was appointed a Board Member of Rowntrees (Figure 11). I held the post of Company Secretary until 1966 when in January Rowntrees became a wholly owned subsidiary of Debenhams Limited.

At that time Rowntrees was experiencing some difficulties with its expansion programme in York that, while feasible would put the company at risk. We were advised that if either of the two main directors, Mr. Ralph Rowntree or Mr. Percy Pickles were to die, many would be put out of work, so the decision was taken to merge with Debenham's in order to safeguard the jobs of over 400 people. This was completed successfully, and the store moved into a new era.

Fig. 11: Members of the Staff Council at the Annual Staff Dinner. Athol J. Wallis is second left in the back row.

*   *   *   *   *

MRS. HILDA GINESI began work at Rowntrees Department Store in 1954 in the Gown Department as 'First Sales' under Miss Lishman.

She tells her story here:

As well as gowns, we had a Fur Department, and it was my job first thing in the morning to wheel the rail of fur coats on to the sales floor, making sure that the chain was threaded through each coat sleeve and fastened securely to the rail, making the garments safe against pilfering.

One day, Mr. P E C Pickles sent for me to attend him in the Board Room, and when I got there, around the table sat Mr.

Ralph Rowntree, Mr. Pickles and Mr. Gilbert. They told me Miss Pearce, the Children's Wear and Lingerie Buyer was retiring and they asked if I would like to take over the position. This was a good opportunity for me, so I accepted.

I found managing the Children's Wear and Lingerie quite easy, but the Corsetry Section was more difficult. However, the store sent me up to London to the Berlei Training School for one week, and at the end of the course I took an examination. The largest model I have ever seen came in and I had to fit her with a back-lacing corset with whalebones and hooks-and-eyes! However, after much tugging and pulling – and with a great deal of help from the lady herself – I passed with flying colours and duly received my diploma as a certified fitter.

Our Children's Department was at the end of the store, down the lovely sweeping staircase. At Christmas time, which started in November, we had the most delightful seasonal displays. One time I recall we had a 'Fairy Grotto' with a tinkling waterfall playing Christmas tunes, and when the children came down the stairs to watch, there were often little pools of water left by the children who couldn't wait to get to the Ladies Room – so the waterfall had to be turned off!

My 'First Sales' on Underwear was a kind gentle soul called Miss Rowe. First Sales in the Children's Section was Mrs. Gladys Bielby, wife of our Electrical Buyer, Harry Bielby. Sometimes I also had to go through to the York store and

Fig. 12: Members of the Oriel Dramatic Club in costume.

79

team up with Miss Foster. We often went to London on buying trips and these were most enjoyable.

The store had a drama group known as the 'Oriel Dramatic Club', to which I belonged, and we would present little plays to the staff (Figure 12). Mr. Edward 'Ted' Neighbour, the Scarborough Store Manager and Eric Mason, Promotions Manager, coached us, and they were quite hilarious. The plays were often staged in St. Saviour's Church Hall, in Gladstone Road, and one I recall, was *When We Are Married* by J B Priestley, which we staged on 28/29 April 1949 (Figure 13). Some of the players included, Paul Temple, Jack Fryer, Peter Bowman – who worked in the Electrical department from 1949-50, Doris Simpson and Mrs. Boden. Ted Neighbour was the producer. Another play we staged was *Sit Down a Minute Adrian.*

Fig. 13: When We Are Married, 1949.
Cast members include
(l - r) Paul Temple, Jack Fryer, Peter Bowman.
Seated (l - r) Doris Simpson, Miss Bowden, unknown.

Fig. 14: Scarborough Open Air Theatre.

*   *   *   *   *

MRS. ETHEL NUNN, of Livingstone Road, worked in the China Department of Rowntrees from 1928 until 1933.

She recalls:

Rowntrees was a very elegant store in those days. Ordinary items were sold like pudding basins, mixing bowls, etc, but the selection of china and cut glass was superb. There was a showcase full of Royal Worcester, and I could have bought a cup and saucer for two pounds – but this meant a month's wages for an apprentice!

Other showcases displayed Royal Doulton, Dresden and Crown Derby. Lalique glass was sold, and about 1931 Clarice Cliff designed some very colourful and decorative earthenware – something quite different. Customer's reactions to the new style of crockery differed widely – some loved it, others hated it, thinking it dreadful. Jug and basin sets comprising five pieces were sold, but only four were ever put on display – the chamber

pot was never displayed, but was kept hidden away in the base-
ment!

One of the highlights of the year was 'Cricket Week',
when all the good shops and stores set out their best merchandise
for the many visitors to the town. Our Department would sometimes borrow a table and linen from another Department and
display a beautiful dinner service with cut glass wine goblets.

I remember Mr. William S. Rowntree, who wore a distinc-
tive Quaker hat and his son, Howard – they were good employers.
They gave us an Annual Staff Outing. One year we went to
Edinburgh, setting off by train at seven o'clock in the morning.
We paid a small amount and Rowntrees arranged the train and
provided the meals and outings to the Forth Road Bridge, Holy-
rood House and other interesting places. Most of us had never
been to Scotland before, so it was very special. For several years
Rowntrees closed their store on August Bank Holiday, but then it
was decided to open as it was such a busy day.

Two young ladies from Rowntrees became 'Rose Queens'
– Rosemary Kidd and Ida Edwards, who later married Les Apple-
by, manager of the garage.

Customers were always the most important consideration.
I remember Charles Laughton visiting the Soft Furnishing Department. We dared not stand, stare or ask for an autograph, but
we managed to get quickly to the edge of the department to have
a brief glimpse of him and his wife, Elsa Lanchester.[3] Elsie and
Doris Waters also visited the store when they were appearing at
the *Floral Hall*. They were both dressed in knitted silk suits and
wearing little round hats to match in the same style as those they
wore in their act. They were very elegant pleasant ladies. On one
occasion shock waves went through the store when a famous
jockey took his wife into the Fur Department and bought not one
but *two* very expensive fur coats!

All female staff had to wear stockings, even in summer; no
bare legs were allowed. Nor was it permissible for staff to call
each other by our Christian names, even out of customer's hearing!

Rhoda Heap in our Department had a fine soprano voice and was in the Open Air Theatre production of *Hiawatha*, playing the lead part of Minnehaha, which was a real achievement for her as all the other parts were played by professionals.

Rowntrees was a good company to work for. Typically, any staff off ill always received a gift of fruit.

There was a Staff Council made up of representatives from each section of the store. They met monthly and concerned themselves with staff welfare.

The store ran a Progressive Management System, a group to which members were elected by the staff and which studied suggestions to improve the efficiency of the store. If a suggestion was accepted, ten shillings or a pound was given to the person who made the suggestion.

Around 1964, Messrs Edward Neighbour and Eric Mason formed 'Young Rowntrees'. Young people were specially invited to this exclusive club and received treats.

The company also ran the *Oriel Sports & Social Club* (Figures 15 & 16) where hockey, tennis, cricket and other sports were played on the Oriel Crescent Sports Ground, and each year

Fig. 15: Oriel Amateur Athletics Social Club Committee, about 1949. (Back, l - r) E. W. Neighbour, Lloyd Wilson, Peter Bowman, Wally Gaunt, George Richardson. (Front, l - r) Joy Mollekin, Ann Rollet, Brenda Clague.

Fig. 16: Staff of Rowntrees at the Oriel Crescent Sports Ground, *c.* 1920.

an inter-store sports competition was held between the Scarborough and York Department Stores.

The Department Store of W Rowntree & Son was finally demolished in 1990, and the site was eventually developed as the current *Brunswick Centre*, containing a branch of Debenhams Plc which had taken over the company of Rowntrees some years earlier.

*   *   *   *   *

Notes and References

1.   Mrs. Jean Wallington attended Scarborough Girls' High School.
2.   Administrative Director and Company Secretary.
3.   Charles Laughton, whose family and himself where born and bred in Scarborough, and had hotel and brewery interests here, lived with his wife Elsa Lanchester for a period in the village of Scalby.

Chapter 7

The Early Lifeboat Service at Scarborough

THE SCARBOROUGH LIFEBOAT STATION is one of the long-est serving stations in the records of the lifeboat service.

In 1800, nearly a quarter of a century before the Royal National Lifeboat Institution itself was founded, a lifeboat was built at Scarborough from the 'plan and moulds' of Henry Great-head, together with instructions for building her, furnished to Mr. Thomas Hinderwell, ship-owner and historian, of Scarborough, 'for a compliment of five guineas'. 'No deviation from that plan or moulds was made in building that boat.' The boat was built and supported by voluntary subscriptions and donations. Among the liberal donors were Earl Fitzwilliam £100, Lord Middleton £100, Mrs. Langley, Bielby Thompson, Esq., and William Joseph Den-nison, Esq., each £50.

In a copy (in the possession of the local secretary) of the *Sun* newspaper published in London, dated 16 December 1801, there is a graphic account written by Thomas Hinderwell of a service by this lifeboat on 2 November 1801, when she rescued the crew of seven from the *Aurora* of Newcastle, going out 'in such a tremendous storm and agitated seas, that no ordinary boat could have hoped to save them.'

Less than three weeks later, on 21 November, the lifeboat was again out on service, saving the crew of seven from a ship in difficulty, and in the following January she saved the *Experiment* of London with her crew of eight.

A second lifeboat for Scarborough was built in 1822. When the Royal National Lifeboat Institution was founded in 1824 there were two boats stationed at Scarborough. This second lifeboat capsized on the 17 February 1836, with the loss of ten lives. The lifeboat house was erected near the Mill Beck, which was underneath the present Spa Bridge. In 1826 the lifeboat house was removed to the present site opposite the slipway adjoining the West Pier.

In 1825 Mr. Skelton built another lifeboat from a design by Mr. Peake. She was 'copper fastened and eight rowers and two steersmen formed the boat's crew.'

A contemporary copy of the *Illustrated London News* gives an account of a service rendered on 17 January 1857, when the lifeboat commanded by Thomas Claybourn succeeded in rescuing the crews of two Whitby vessels and, on another occasion, the crew of nine of the *Wilsons*.

One of the crew of the life-boat, Thomas Luccock, was thrown out of the boat, and had a narrow escape; 'his life-belt was no doubt his preserver.'

This lifeboat, however, was considered too small, so a local committee applied to the Royal National Lifeboat Institution, which resulted in a gift from a Mr. Banting of London in April 1861, of a larger boat called the *Amelia*.

In that year the operation of the Scarborough lifeboat station was taken over by the Royal National Lifeboat Institution.

In September 1861 the *Amelia* was disabled by being dashed against the sea wall of the Spa, while endeavouring to rescue the crew of the schooner *Coupland*, which was wrecked in front of the Spa. Two of the crew of the lifeboat, John Burton and Thomas Brewster, were thrown out of the boat and drowned. A crowd of spectators rushed down the incline to save the rest of the crew when a huge wave swept several people into the sea, and Lord Charles Beauclerc, William Tindall, and John Iles were drowned.

The disabled boat was replaced by a new one called the *Mary*, through the generosity of Mrs. Cockcroft, a local resident.

This boat was at Scarborough until September 1872, she was replaced with the *Lady Leigh*, presented by the Freemasons of Warwickshire, Lord Leigh being the Provincial Grand Master of the Province of Warwick at the time.

The *Lady Leigh* was at the station until 1887, and from 1872 to 1887 she had been instrumental in the saving of one hundred and six lives. She was subsequently replaced by the first of three boats, all named *Queensbury*, presented and endowed by Colonel Herbert Foster of Queensbury Works, Bradford, and members of his family. These three lifeboats served at Scarborough consecutively from 1887 to 1918, with the exception of the years 1901 and 1902, when a temporary boat was in use while the second Queensbury boat was awaiting replacement. The Lifeboat Service records for this period are:

> *Queensbury* (1887-1895) launched twenty-one times. Lives rescued thirty-five.
> *Queensbury* (1895-1901) launched fifteen times. Lives rescued eight.
> Temporary Boat (1901-1902) launched five times. Lives rescued sixteen.
> *Queensbury* (1902-1918) launched sixty times. Lives rescued ninety-eight.

From 1918 to 1923 a reserve lifeboat named the *Brother Brickwood* was stationed at Scarborough, and was launched twenty-seven times and rescued fifty-five lives.

In 1923 a specially light motor life-boat of a new type, designed to be launched from a carriage run on to the beach, was presented to the Scarborough branch of the Royal National Life-

Fig. 1: Storm damage in Scarborough after Gales, 12 March 1906

boat Institution by Mr. Alexander O. Joy, in memory of his brother Herbert Joy, who was drowned in Scarborough Bay. The boat was named the *Herbert Joy*.

In 1931 this boat was replaced, again through the generosity of Mr. Alexander O. Joy, by the *Herbert Joy II*, which was christened by H.R.H. the Princess Royal on 3 August 1931.

One famous name that will always be linked with the early history of the Scarborough lifeboat is John Owston, the late coxswain, who retired in 1912, after being coxswain of the Scarborough lifeboat for forty-one years.

He received a pension, a special gratuity, and a certificate of service. He won the silver medal for gallantry in October 1880, when in the course of a little over twenty-four hours, with a terrible gale blowing, the lifeboat was launched no fewer than five times to vessels in distress, and rescued every life in danger on board them – twenty-eight in all.

Altogether Owston took part in the rescue of two hundred and thirty lives. In 1902 King Edward VII presented him with two silver-mounted pipes.

When John Owston retired, he was succeeded by his son, John Owston. The son was endowed with the same courage and spirit of service as the father. This is particularly exemplified in a rescue which he effected in August 1918:

> *At 8.10 am on Saturday the 10 of August 1918, the lifeboat coxswain, John Owston, who was going to his boat in the harbour, received intimation from a harbour official that a vessel had just been torpedoed in the North Bay. On behalf of the Lifeboat Institution, the coxswain immediately instructed the motor boat Ypres (master, Frank Boynton, second coxswain of the Filey Lifeboat) to go out to the vessel, and got on board himself.*
>
> *The master of the motor boat ran on petrol the whole time and quickly reached the scene of the disaster. A passing cargo-boat, Tyneside, had rushed to the spot and lowered a boat and picked up four of the crew of the torpedoed vessel. As the motor boat had not a small boat on board and there was difficulty in manoeuvring her to the men in the water, the coxswain took off his sea-boots (he had no life-belt on), jumped overboard, and brought two of the men to the motor boat in an exhausted state. The motorboat picked up another man and the cargo-boat transferred the four they had saved to the motorboat and proceeded on her voyage. Ten of the crew of the torpedoed vessel were lost, and that number might well have been increased to twelve if it had not been for the prompt action of the lifeboat coxswain.*

Sometime later, in 1928, it was fitting that John Owston's daughter, Olive, a scholar of Gladstone Road School, won the Duke of

Northumberland's lifeboat essay competition for the best essay in the north-eastern area on 'What a Lifeboat Man should be.'

There are no records of the number of lives saved by Scarborough lifeboats from 1800 to 1861, but since the RNLI took over the Scarborough station, the Scarborough lifeboats have rescued from shipwrecks over three hundred and sixty people, and twelve silver medals have been awarded by the institution to men of this station for personal gallantry in life-saving.

Fig. 2: The launching of a Scarborough lifeboat.

AN EYE-WITNESS ACCOUNT OF A RESCUE BY LIFEBOAT

"ON 25 June 1919 Mr. V Feather was in Scarborough and spending the evening at the open-air concert on the Spa. The evening was fine in the sense of being dry, but there was a strong northerly wind increasing towards a gale, and he withdrew his attention from the music to observe the situation of a schooner, which earlier in the day had been left by her tug at anchor off Carnelian Bay.

"As the gale increased it seemed that every time the vessel reared to a breaking sea she dragged her anchor slightly towards the shore, and that within a few hours at most she would strike the rocky bottom and break up. 'I felt the incongruous position of the audience, enjoying the concert, and not knowing that close at hand were men in peril and powerless to help themselves.'

"When it became dusk I began to feel impatient with those men for not signalling for help before dark. It was obvious they could do nothing to preserve their ship, but they stoutly hung on until daylight was just ending, and then they hoisted the ensign half-way to the peak and burned a red flare over the quarter rail.'

"The signals were answered at once by the lifeboat station, and within a few minutes the lifeboat was launched and on its way. It seemed a small, frail craft as it rose on the crests and sank out of sight in the troughs, and though it made rapid progress under its oars, I wondered how it would fare in the smother of broken seas where the

schooner leaped and plunged, and how manpower could bring it back head into the gale.'

"Darkness now came, and the crowd on the piers and foreshore could only wait for the return of the boat to know whether a complete rescue had been made. The suspense was tense but short, and as the lifeboat entered the harbour someone hailed to ask whether all were saved. The reply, 'Aye, we've got 'em all!' produced heartfelt cheers from everybody.'

"I learned that the schooner was the Melba of Newcastle, with a crew of eight, and that the speedy return of the lifeboat under such conditions was due to the coxswain having double-banked the oars with the rescued crew. I imagine that those men certainly would have put their backs into it.'

"At daybreak I looked for the schooner, but there was no sign that she had existed."

This incident is but one in the long service record of the Scarborough lifeboat, and though it did not involve the long period of physical exposure called for in less spectacular duties in wintertime, it was nevertheless a case where the peril was imminent to both rescuers and rescued, and should be regarded as typical of the regular work of the RNLI.

A 19th century lifeboatman wearing a cork life-jacket.

Chapter 8

The Spaw Years

. . . Scarborough boasts
A double portion of the healing strength
In her famed Spaw, that treasures all its stores.
Where yonder roof, erected on the waves.
Grotesquely lurks beneath the pendant cliff.

THE SPAW HOUSE of olden times was firstly a little wood hut and primitive buildings in which the nobility and gentry who visited Scarborough were wont to assemble for the purpose of drinking the mineral waters served to them in drinking-horns by old women, who with aid of cups fitted to the end of long wands so as to reach into the wells to extract the mineral water.

The fame of these waters has been known for centuries. The credit for discovering their properties is attributed to a lady named Mrs. Farrow in 1620.

The first cistern for collecting the waters was made in 1698.

In 1737 the old Spaw House and other parts of the town were destroyed by an earthquake and it was rebuilt in 1739.

This event prompted a sermon to be preached on 28 December 1737, the text being from Isaiah XXVI, 9 – 'When Thy judgements are in the earth, the inhabitants of the world will learn righteousness.'

A superintendent, formally entitled 'the Governor of the Spaw', was appointed by the Corporation, to attend to the receiving of subscriptions, and to preserve order in regulating each ward, and distinction of apartments.

The Old Spa had several Governors, the most famous of whom was 'Dicky' Dickinson, who flourished about the year 1725, and died at a good old age on 8 February 1738.

Mr. William Templeton, Governor, died 12 January 1755.

Mr. William Allanson lived to the age of 103 years, and died in 1775. Whenever he was questioned about his mode of living he invariably answered "that he had always lived well, and the Spaw-water was his sovereign remedy". He retained all his faculties to the last.

Mr. Thomas Headley, Governor, died in 1701. He was a man of great civility, and unexceptional conduct, which was far more than could be said of many of his predecessors.

Mr. James Pearson, another Governor, died in 1821. In his former life he endured much suffering in shipwrecks, and ended his days as Governor of the Spaw.

The rebuilt Spaw House of 1739.

In 1787 the subscriptions to the Spaw were seven shillings and sixpence for each person who drank the water – two shillings and sixpence of which went to the women who served it, and five shillings was received by the Corporation towards reimbursing their heavy expenses in building, repairing, and supporting the Spaw house, platform and walk.

The very general use and widely extended fame of these waters in olden times, owed much to strong recommendations from the great Dr. Mead, among whose patients such great benefit was derived as to make them exceedingly popular.

A traditional account records that several neighbouring gentlemen and others, who were Royalists, having assisted in defending the Castle of Scarborough against Sir John Meldrum and the Parliamentary forces, suffered much contracted scurvy from long confinement and unwholesome food but, after drinking the waters of this spring, they completely recovered very soon.

A severe gale and an unusually high tide occurred on the 17 February 1836, which were so powerful that the Old Spaw, Staith and several other buildings were entirely destroyed, and required rebuilding and enlargement.

An engraving depicts the appearance of the Spaw and cliff before its destruction by the storm and shows a striking contrast to the 'palace of beauty and fairy-like surroundings brought about by the masterly hand' of Sir Joseph Paxton who rebuilt them.

The medical properties of these celebrated Spa waters were first brought to public notice about the year 1620 by Mrs. Farrow, a resident of Scarborough.

She sometimes walked this way, and observing the stones over which the water passed to have taken on a russet colour, and finding it to have an acid taste, different from the common springs, and to receive a purple tincture from galls, supposed the waters might have medical property. Therefore, having conducted an experiment herself, and persuaded others to do the same, she was found it to be efficacious in the treatment of some complaints, and became the usual medicine of the inhabitants.

It was later held in great repute by the citizens of York and the gentry of the county and at length was so generally recommended that several persons of quality came from a great distance to drink it, preferring it before all the others at spas they had formerly frequented, even those in Italy, France, and Germany.

Dr. Granville, the noted Spa tourist, pronounced Scarborough one of the most interesting marine Spas in England.

The celebrated 'Dicky' Dickinson, an original character, was the first Governor of Scarborough Spaw.

His body was very deformed but he possessed an uncommonly brilliant wit and considerable ingenuity. The man's eccentricity was known to most of the poets, wits and painters of the last century, and the singularity of his figure contributed to bring him into the attention of the gentry and others who visited the Scarborough Spaw, where he resided as governor and, in addition, followed the dual occupation of shoe cleaner and vendor of gingerbread.

He was one of those beings whom Nature, in one of her sportive moods, formed and sent into the world to prove the great variety of her works.

Though he had arms and legs like other men, they were, however, so strangely deformed as to make him the object of both admiration and laughter.

'Dicky' was never at a loss for an answer to any joke that might be levelled at him and, with a quaintness of manner peculiarly to himself, was ever certain of raising a laugh at the expense of his antagonists. A facetious writer says: "There ought to be a promoter of innocent mirth at every watering-place, for the exhilaration of invalids," and observes, "An ass that brayed so as to convulse them with laughter, would to these people be of more real use than ten asses laden with drugs".

There are no less than seven original portrayals of Dicky Dickinson produced by different artists. The best portrait is said to be by Hysing, dated 1725. On a mezzotint of Dickinson, copied from Vertue's print, is inscribed the following:

Behold the Governor of Scarborough Spaw,
The strangest phiz and form you ever saw,
Yet when you view the beauties of his mind,
In him a second Æsop you may find.
Samos unenvied boasts her Æsop gone,
And France may glory in her late Scarron,
While England has her living Dickinson.

The celebrated
'Dicky' Dickinson.

A full-length etching of Dickinson bears the imposing title, *The exact Effigies of Dicky Dickinson, commonly called 'King Dicky' Governor of the Privy Houses of Scarborow Spaw, whose ingenuity, industry, and expense, in contriving and building conveniences for gentlemen and ladies is worthy of notice, and of no small advantage to Scarborow.* It was drawn from life by a gentleman who had the advantage of a year's observation of Dicky's most natural posture and countenance.

Under another etching, drawn by the same gentleman, representing Dickinson in a sitting posture, is written:

King 'Dicky' thus seated his subjects to greet,
With scurvy jokes treats them, and fancy's they're wit,
Then laughs 'til the rheum runs down from both eyes,
To his grizzled beard, which the drivel supplies,
And like to old Sydrophel, fain would seem wise.

The following account of this Scarborough celebrity of the eighteenth century appears in *Le Magasin Pictouresque of Paris*:

Richard Dickinson flourished at Scarborough Spaw about the year 1725. Verses were composed and printed in honour of him, and he received the title of the English Scarron. Hysing painted his portrait, and Vertue engraved it. What claim then had this man to such celebrity? None except the ugliness of his countenance, and the deformity of his body. The fashionable loungers who spent the summer at Scarborough Spaw, found a melancholy amusement in laughing at his expense; but at least they did not forget to generously reward the poor fellow's gambols and grimaces. They paid him so well, indeed, that a day came when Dickinson found himself rich enough to open a little shop. Henceforth he refused to become the sport of anyone.

By dint of hard work and severe economy he grew to be almost a wealthy man, while some of the rakes who used to insult him by their railleries fell off by degrees into poverty and degradation, and envied his prosperity when they passed his door. Here we have a curious example of the strange turns of the wheel of fortune.

The contributor of the above article had in his possession a curious relic of the renowned Dickinson. It is a walking stick with a carved human head, with a long chin, hanging beard and a cap, said to be a likeness of Dickinson.

Dicky being of a very lively demeanour, his society was much enjoyed by visitors to the Spaw.

On one occasion a lady visitor, being fascinated either by the charms or the peculiarities of Dicky, offered her hand and heart to the 'potentate of the waters', which was met by an ungallant and bluff refusal on his part, accompanied by the declaration that he would not have her, as she was too much like his clock.

"Why am I like your clock?" inquired the lady, with feminine, but pardonable, inquisitiveness.

"Because," replied the Governor, "she is always too forward, and so I think are you."

The remark afterwards came into general, local usage: 'You are like the Spaw clock,' and was used in Scarborough for many years after to chide people who were impertinent or poked their noses into other people's business.

The following lines were also written on the character of this celebrated individual, and were affixed to the margin of one of his portraits:

> *A mighty Monarch, here I reign,*
> *And lord it over land and main;*
> *Both sea and land their tribute bring,*
> *And both conspire to prove me king.*
> *The sea itself does twice a day*
> *Advance and homage to me pay;*
> *Yet some infer like sons of whores,*
> *Neptune's grown jealous of our powers,*
> *Turns me and Peggy out of doors;*
> *Because he once or twice a year,*
> *Within my palace dare appear.*

Whereas the good old God prepares
Only to wash my hall and stairs.
This wondrous infant shall not raise
From arms or politics his praise;
No crown or sceptre, no, nor mace,
His head or hand shall ever grace,
Yet shall my Dicky's favourite name
Shine foremost in the list of fame;
I'll make him Sovereign of the Spaw,
To keep the squirting tribe in awe,
The loosest shall obey his law.
Nor shall he ever want a wile
To make fools laugh, or ladies smile.

The Legend of 'Dicky' Dickinson.

'Quaint 'Dicky' Dickinson lived long ago,
In Scarborough town, as all may know;
He was a king and he gave the law,
Governor over the ancient 'Spaw.'
Quaint 'Dicky' Dickinson turned to dust,
As every king and governor must;
There he lay, and there he lay,
For many a year, till an autumn day;
The dust was stirred with a trembling air,
For the ghost that had lived in the dust was there.
Back 'Dicky' Dickinson came to the earth,
To see the place of his mortal birth,
For he had longed, in a distant star,
Where the souls of kings and governors are,
Had longed again on the shore to be,
And hear the surge of the Northern sea;
To stand on the "Spaw", where he gave the law,
And to know if any were held as he.

Quaint 'Dicky' Dickinson said to his dust,
'Lie thou there, till meet we must.'
Quaint 'Dicky' Dickinson said to himself,
'Faith, but it is a forgotten shelf!'
Straight to the 'Spaw' he took his way,
Went over the Bridge, and did not pay;
The ticket collector felt a blast
As 'Dicky' the Governor's ghost went past.
Down the walks and the colonnade –
Swiftly out on the promenade –
Up to the 'band where the music plays,'
And the lighted lamps are all ablaze!
He sat at the top of the chandelier,
And he said, 'It is mighty-remarkably queer!'
He perched on the bow of the First Violin,
And he said, 'Pray when does the ball begin?'
But his wordless whispering only made
A quivering chord as the air was played.
He stood on the tower, and so looked down
Over the 'Spaw' and across at the town.

Glittering, glistening, gliding about,
Backwards and forwards, within and without;
Lamps, and ladies, and flowers so rare,
Duns after dandies all taking the air;
Hat, and feather, and dear little head –
How it bewilders a man who is dead!
Train, and cloak, and dangling beau –
Backwards and forwards, and hither and fro;
Half by the lamps-half by the moon,
As if they were all stirred up with a spoon.

Then 'Dicky' the Governor sighed and said,
'The world goes on though I am dead.
Ay me! In their jovial glee

Who ever thinks of a ghost like me?
He saw the 'Crown,' and he saw the 'Grand,'
And he saw the streets stretch far inland;
His heart cried out for the years gone by,
And he fain would speak, but could only sigh.
'Fair, fair, and full of fame,
But Scarborough town is not the same:
Where is the "Spaw," where I gave the law?
And nought did lack but a kingly name?
There is but the sea that knoweth me,
With the Church and Castle that by it be;
This is not the world where I did reign,
Better go back to the dead again!'

Apart from the Spaw, private enterprise equipped several establishments for the convenience of the sick and disabled and others who were prevented from bathing in the sea with much elegance and comfort in Scarborough. Among them may be mentioned Dr. Travis's Baths that stood at the corner of St. Nicholas Cliff entrance.

These baths were originally opened in 1798, and rebuilt in 1822. The tubs were made of wood and marble, and adapted for plunging, sitting or lying in. At each tide, they were refreshed with pure sea water. They were also fitted with a steam room, douche and showers.

Weddell's Baths were situated near to the outer Pier, and were erected in 1812.

Harland's Baths were built in New Road, at the bottom of Vernon Place.

Champley's baths occupied a position in Cockerill's Garden, nearly central between the Cliff and Belvoir Terrace, and contained a suite for ladies and another for gentlemen.

In 1829, Mrs. Vickerman also had some baths built on the sand near to the Marine Houses, at the foot of King Street Steps.

All these buildings were later either pulled down or converted for other purposes.

Travis's Bath, near the Cliff.

Weddell's Baths, near the Pier.

Harland's Baths, near Vernon Place.

Champley's Baths.

In 1732, a writer of a letter describing the bathing season at Scarborough, says:

> *It is the custom for not only the gentlemen, but the ladies also, to bath[e] in the sea: the gentlemen go out a little way to sea in boats (called here cobles) and jump in naked directly. The ladies have the convenience of gowns and guides. There are two little houses on the shore, to retire for dressing in. What virtues our physicians ascribe to cold baths in general, are much more effectual by the additional weight of salt in sea-water; an advantage which no Spaw in England can boast of but Scarborough!*

An ingenious gentleman who, from his sketch of this place, seems very well acquainted with it, tells of a friend of his who, seeing the ladies bathing in the sea – whole groups of them at a time – among whom was Pastorella (the lady of his affections), inspired by so unusual a sight, broke out into the following lines:

> *D'you think, what ancient Bards suppose,*
> *That Venus from the Ocean rose,*
> *Before she did ascend the Skies,*
> *To dwell among the Deities.*
>
> *Yes sure: Why not? Since here you see*
> *Nymphs full as beautiful as she,*
> *Emerging daily from the Sea.*
>
> *The Nymph that captivates my Love,*
> *Gay Pastorella, there, will prove,*
> *That her Perfections cannot die:*
> *She in her turn will mount the Sky,*
> *And reign the lovelier Deity.*

During the eighteenth century bathing was as popular with the visitors to Scarborough as it was in the following century, though the facilities for indulging in this luxury were probably not so great.

In 1787, long before the bathing machines were under the control of old Betty Liddle, Messrs. Southwell, Chapman, Richardson, Morrison, Crosby, Brown, Walshaw, or Fowler, there were about twenty-six large and commodious bathing machines drawn out every morning on the Sands for the service of the company. They belonged to three different proprietors who usually solicited strangers on their early arrival to patronise their respective vehicles. Their names were Fields, Hunter and Laycock.

Two women usually attended each lady who bathed, as guides and one man to provide the service for each gentleman who required it. A lad attended with a horse to pull the machine to and from the water, and to any depth the bather pleased. The horse was then uncoupled and the machine left until she or he had finished bathing. On a pre-arranged signal, the lad would return and draw the machine back to its former station.

The regular price for bathing was one shilling each time for the hire of the machine. At the completion of a bathing session a gratuity was usually bestowed on the guides and the lad who conducted the machine, as a recompense for the uncomfortable, fatiguing, amphibious life they led, and as a reward for their – in general – very civil attention.

Bathing on the Sands was often a source of great pleasure and excitement to the promenaders. A Mr. Austin who wrote about that time described it thus:

> *" Of all the fine sights*
> *I never expect to behold such another;*
> *How the ladies set up their clacks,*
> *All the while an old woman was rubbing their backs; -*

O! 'twas pretty to see them put on their flannels,
And then take to the water, like so many spaniels;
While Tabby —
In spite of good company — poor little soul,
Shook both her ears like a mouse in a bowl.

The proposed Sea-bathing Infirmary for the Poor.

Chapter 9

Shipwrecks off the
Scarborough Coast

T HE FORTUNES OF THE TOWN OF SCARBOROUGH have always been very closely bound up with the sea; indeed it is thought the earliest recorded settlement here was made by people who came from the sea and not from inland.

An early representation of a shipwreck.

Skarthi, the Viking, landed here in the year 966 AD and founded a settlement known as *Skarthiburgh*, from which the town's present name was probably derived. Scarborough is dominated by a huge headland known as Scarborough Rock, which has long been an important strategic position.

A Roman signal station was built here as an early warning system against raids from the Saxons and Scandinavians in the fourth century AD.

Later, the strong defensive qualities of the rock were noted by the Norman king, Henry II, in whose reign the first Scarborough Castle was established in 1157. This castle was visited at various times by at least three English kings and it withstood no less than six sieges over the centuries, the most important being during the Civil War of 1644-45.

The Rock effectively divides the town into two distinct parts with a well-defined bay at each side. The focal point of the area is Scarborough harbour, built at the southern foot of the Castle Cliff during the twelfth century.

Fig. 1: Scarborough Lighthouse

This is not the place for a detailed history of the harbour, (Figure 1) but records show that by 1336 ten boats belonged to Scarborough, all of 40-50 tons burden. During the fourteenth century, trade with Holland, France, Norway and Germany had already begun, with imports mainly of timber, pitch and wax. In 1565 the burgesses of Scarborough said, *'Theare is no other save harbours betwixt Humber and Tyne but onelie Skarburghe.'*
Today hardly any cargo vessels put in at Scarborough, but in summer time short sea trips are run up and down the coast for the enjoyment of holidaymakers, but Scarborough is, first and foremost, a fishing port as it has always been. (Figure 2)

Fig. 2: Fisher girls at work packing herrings on the harbourside

The keel boats used for fishing today are powerful purpose-built vessels, far from elegant in appearance, but having a beauty of their own. Equipped as they are with thousands of pounds worth of electronic aids, it is now rare for one of these splendid vessels to come to grief, but this has not always been the case.

113

Before the advent of steam trawlers, the traditional fishing vessels of Scarborough were yawls and smacks, used for line fishing and trawling respectively. These too were beautiful vessels, and it was said that in bad weather a fishing smack under sail could outpace even the finest racing yacht.

Smacks were usually of sixty tons or so and timber built, though steel was increasingly used in the construction of some later vessels. They carried a crew of up to eleven men and were usually at sea for weeks at a time, covering quite amazing distances.

The yawls tended to be smaller, though it was quite common for a yawl to be converted into a smack (the difference was principally in the rig of the vessels).

Many of the Scarborough owned smacks had been built in the town, but others came from Whitby, Grimsby, Lowestoft and various yards from around the coast.

During the forty years between 1859 and 1899 more than sixty of these vessels set out on fishing trips never to return and, in most of these cases, they were lost with all hands. Only too numerous are the reports in the *Scarborough Gazette* which read, "All hope has been given up for the smack. . . of this port, which sailed for the fishing grounds on the . . ."

A few weeks later a subscription would be opened by some local benefactor and the sums donated to the ten or eleven widows and twenty or more children would be listed with agonising accuracy.

One particularly unhappy time for the Scarborough fishing fraternity was during the storms of October 1869, when 31 men were lost in three smacks that foundered at sea.

A public meeting was held at which it was reported that the loss sustained by Scarborough and Filey amounted to £20,000 as a result of one storm.

Another tragedy of this kind occurred in December 1883 when three more smacks were lost with all hands. As the 47-ton *Intrepid* began to sink, the 46-ton *Queen of England* came alongside to take off her crew. Heavy seas smashed the craft together, as a result of which both crews and both vessels went to the bottom.

Ten days later, on 22 December 1883, the 62-ton *Empress* also foundered with all hands.

Most of the shipwrecks which occurred in the Scarborough area in the days of sailing vessels, were as a result of bad weather combined with the hostility of the shore. When a gale sprang up, masters of passing vessels had to decide whether to stay offshore and risk the possibility of springing a leak or to run for the harbour and rely on their skill to gain its safety.

More often than not they stayed offshore until they were on the point of sinking and then made a desperate attempt to reach port.

One of the earliest recorded losses of this kind occurred on 9 February 1799, when an unnamed Newcastle brigantine came ashore in Scarborough South Bay in a north-easterly blizzard. She was one of an ill-fated convoy from the Baltic that had been harassed and scattered by days of continuous bad weather off the Yorkshire coast.

The crew of the brigantine were fortunate in escaping with their lives having struggled ashore exhausted after the vessel ran aground.

Many are the stories that could be told of the storms that visited Scarborough, but space allows only a brief mention of some of these.

Six vessels were wrecked in a north-easterly gale on 24 November 1821, with the loss of many lives and several more came to grief during storms in October 1824.

One of the worst lifeboat disasters Yorkshire has seen occurred here on 25 February 1836, when ten men drowned while attempting to save the crew of the sloop *John of Aberdeen,* which grounded and was wrecked in the South Bay.

Ironically, perhaps, the three crew of the sloop were brought safely ashore by the use of Captain Manby's patent rocket apparatus.

Four more sailing ships were wrecked here in an easterly gale on 4 January 1857, and less than four years later Scarborough's best-known shipwreck occurred in the South Bay.

The South Shields schooner *Coupland*, laden with a cargo of granite, was attempting to enter the harbour during a violent gale on 2 November 1861.

On rounding the pier at 4 pm she was taken aback, her sails disabled, and the vessel began to drift helplessly towards the cruel rocks at the south end of the bay.

Eventually, the heavy surf picked her up and she was carried along at a frightening rate until she struck with a grinding crunch, coming to rest some thirty yards from the sea wall were her crew, though uncomfortable, were not in imminent danger of drowning.

The lifeboat, a new one named *Amelia*, was manned and launched in an effort to take off the stranded seamen, but the surf proved too much for her and she quickly ran into problems of her own.

The *Amelia* was picked up by the breakers and hurled against the sea wall. One of her crew was pitched overboard. His cork life jacket saved him and he struggled ashore where a large crowd had gathered.

The lifeboat's oars were lost, and the crew were thrown from the boat one by one as the surf tossed her about. One lifeboatman was crushed to death between the sea wall and the lifeboat, and another was drowned. The remainder managed to struggle ashore.

Meanwhile, a crowd of spectators had waded out into the surf to try and reach the lifeboatmen, and three of the would-be rescuers, including Lord Charles Beauclerck, were also swept off their feet and drowned. Thus five lives were lost in the rescue attempt, and yet the six crew of the *Coupland* were finally saved by use of the rocket apparatus that had been set up on the shore.

The *Coupland* became a total wreck, as did the *Amelia*, the new lifeboat of which the townspeople had been so proud.

On the night of 26 October 1869, crowds assembled on the cliffs south of Scarborough to witness a scene described thus by one eye witness:

> *Great foaming waves were dashing against the cliff*
> *. . . the darkness was rent by a great meteor flash*
> *as a rocket rushed blazing out to sea . . . two*
> *hundred yards distant a heavily laden schooner*
> *with a few pitch black sails still set was rolling*
> *fearfully on the rocks. Each successive wave broke*
> *right over the hull . . .*

Unknown to him, the watcher was describing the South Shields schooner *Mary*, which had sprung a leak earlier in the day.

The master had decided to run for the shore and the *Mary* struck the rocks south of the Spa after darkness had fallen. The rocket the witness described failed to reach the wreck, as did the next two that were fired, being driven back by the force of the wind.

A ridiculous situation arose: the rocket brigade ran out of rockets and a rider was sent with all speed to bring more. Meanwhile, a huge bonfire was lit on the cliff top, giving an eerie light to the whole scene as the crew of the *Mary* shouted from the rigging where they had sought safety.

Just before midnight the rockets arrived and, before long, communication with the wreck was achieved. The master and four crew of the *Mary* were finally brought ashore after some hours of agonising waiting.

On 17 December 1869, one vessel that actually struck the cliffs at the castle foot was the barque, *Highbury*, of South Shields. She had been trying to make the port of Shields the previous afternoon, but a violent storm had prevented this. As night fell, Captain Williams decided that the safest course of action was to run for shelter in Bridlington Bay, and this was attempted. At 5 am however, her ballast shifted and the *Highbury* became unmanageable. She finally drove ashore at Scarborough between six and 7 am and immediately keeled over.

The master and six crew members climbed the rigging and were able to jump from the mastheads onto the cliffs, from where they scrambled to safety. Two other crew members stepped over the vessel's quarter to wade ashore, but they were swept away by the breakers and lost. Their bodies were found washed ashore later the same evening.

The *Highbury*, owned by Mr. Holiday of Shields and built of oak, was smashed to pieces before daylight. She had been bound for her home port light at the time of her loss having delivered her cargo in London.

Of the many storms that hit Scarborough over the years, none surpassed the great gale of 1880 when the South Bay was filled with stricken vessels, many of which were smashed to matchwood. The storm broke around noon on Wednesday 27 October and, by first light on Thursday, all the rescue services were ready, watching and waiting for the inevitable victims.

Shortly after eight o'clock in the morning, a brig with tattered sails and broken rigging was seen desperately trying to reach the harbour. Like so many others before her, she failed and was driven ashore by the ESE gale in the middle of the Bay. She struck at 10 am and almost at once the lifeboat was alongside her to take off the crew of six.

The brig proved to be the 210-ton *Mary*, of Shields, bound home in ballast from Newhaven.

Shortly afterwards, the 148-ton schooner *Black-Eyed Susan*, of Appledore, was driven violently ashore under the cliffs south of the Spa. The rocket brigade made contact with her almost as soon as she grounded, but again the storm-tossed lifeboat effected the rescue, bringing the five crew ashore to the ringing cheers of the crowd lining the sea front.

Two more vessels followed in the same way. The brig *Jeune Adolphe,* of Dunkirk, and the brig *Arun,* of Littlehampton, drove ashore and both crews were saved by the rescue services.

Meanwhile, two other vessels were seen apparently racing for the harbour mouth.

First to arrive was the brig *Maria*, of Yarmouth, whose crew managed to get a rope to the pier. For a while it seemed that she might be hauled into the harbour mouth, but a heavy sea struck her and the rope parted like cotton.

Almost at same time, the second vessel, the brigantine *Glastry*, of Maryport, Isle of Wight, smashed into the *Maria* in the harbour mouth. Again ropes were thrown to the pier and this time with success. The *Glastry* was hauled up into the harbour mouth, and for a time she was safe.

Attention was drawn from these events by the appearance of an almost dismasted hulk driving towards the worst rocks at the south end of the bay. She was the 192-ton brig *Lily*, of Guernsey, bound for Shields from London in ballast. Only her foremast remained, supporting a tattered foresail as she drove helplessly onto the rocks like a ghost appearing through the driving rain and the gathering gloom.

Thousands of anxious spectators watched the rocket brigade trying to reach her as darkness descended on the bay. Seven rockets were fired and driven back by the gale, but the eighth fell across the brig and the breeches buoy was set up.

One by one, the crew were brought ashore, and was greeted with a hearty cheer from the crowd as he landed safely. One unfortunate man was suspended halfway between the ship and the shore when the rope came fast, and he was held there for several agonising minutes while the sea raged about him and the rain fell in torrents.

Eventually the rope came free and he was dragged from the surf more dead than alive.

The last of the nine men to reach safety was Captain Boucher, clutching his pet dog to his chest as he was landed in a state of utter exhaustion.

An eyewitness described it as a scene of:

> *Perfect Pandemonium . . . where the wind and sea were raging with unbated violence, where the boiling waters hissed and seethed like a mighty furnace, where stately vessels were driven hither and thither like toys on the relentless breakers rolling mountains high.*

After darkness had fallen, the 70-ton ketch, *J. Prizeman*, of Plymouth came ashore without loss of life and at 3 am the *Glastry* broke her moorings and joined the other stranded vessels in the bay.

Another schooner, the 200-ton *Bosphorus*, added to the confusion but again her crew were saved.

All night the rescue services were kept busy and the following day brought no respite.

As the morning wore on the wind abated and the rain stopped but a tremendous sea was still running.

At noon the Dutch barge *Zwei Gebruder* came ashore and her crew took to the rigging until the lifeboat took them off safely.

By 2 am the worst was over. The sea had fallen considerably and people were able to breathe more easily and take stock of the damage.

No less than ten vessels littered the bay, many of them never to sail again.

News had been received that a Scarborough smack, the 46-ton *General Lee* had been lost at sea with all hands. Three vessels were ashore north of the town and other vessels had been seen to founder off shore.

Amazingly not one life had been lost in the South Bay – a great tribute to the courage and skill of the rescue services.

Thankfully, the town has not been visited by such a devastating storm since that time, though hardly a year passed during the nineteenth century without at least one wreck here as a result of heavy weather.

The latter end of 1901, however, brought back reminders of what these storms could do, and the all too familiar pattern began to emerge again on 13 November. A strong ENE gale was blowing and a tremendous sea was running. When a number of vessels were seen approaching at 6.45 am the lifeboat was prepared.

A Scottish fishing vessel gained the harbour in safety at 7.15 am and the 93-ton Rochester ketch *Invicta* decided to try and do likewise.

When she was less than a mile from the harbour mouth, a huge wave crashed down on her and vanished immediately. Her sudden disappearance was almost unbelievable, but there was no mistake. The *Invicta* had sunk with all hands.

At 9.30 am the 192-ton brigantine *Boxer* came into view, with every shred of canvas torn from her yards. She too missed the harbour mouth and drove ashore in the centre of the South Bay, where the waiting lifeboat saved her eight crew. The *Boxer* was smashed and her wreck was sold for £8 a few days later.

Owned by Holder Gann & Co. of Faversham, she had been built in 1865 at New Brunswick. At the time of her loss she had been bound for Hartlepool from Gravesend in ballast.

Almost exactly the same fate met the 274-ton barque *Satellite* a month later on 14 December 1901. She was seen at 5.30 am making distress signals a mile east of the harbour and with her sails gone. The gale drove her onto the beach at 7 am where she was met by the stalwart lifeboatmen, who landed the crew of eight in safety.

Their rescue task was made more difficult by the wreckage of the *Boxer* which was lashing around dangerously in the turbulent sea.

When the tide receded, the *Satellite* was left high and dry on the beach with her hull undamaged, looking for all the world as if she might easily be saved. It was not to be however; subsequent heavy seas battered the vessel until she was sold for £110 where she lay as a wreck. A local fishmonger bought her and made a handsome profit by selling the ropes and equipment to local seamen.

The *Satellite* was owned by Filmer C. Baldwin of Dover and had been bound light for Hartlepool under the command of Captain Robert Dunn when she was lost.

The next notable shipping loss in the South Bay occurred during World War I, when the 3,099-ton steamer *Trelyon* became a victim of German aggression.

On 21 July 1917, some three miles north of Scarborough, she was shaken from stem to stern by a violent explosion, presumably caused by a mine. After the explosion the *Trelyon* did not sink, but was taken in tow by local steamers and was beached at White Nab, the southernmost point of Scarborough's South Bay. She remained there for more than three months, during which time a vast area of the sea was covered with the timber she had brought from Archangel.

Local fishing boats were kept busy for some time gathering the wood and landing it at Scarborough.

On 3 October, tugs brought the wreck to the harbour mouth to the horror of the Scarborough Harbour Commissioners. The 323 ft. long wreck constituted a serious hazard to navigation and eventually the Board of Trade set salvage operations in motion.

It was nearly five years before the *Trelyon* had been dispersed sufficiently well to satisfy the Commissioners.

The last large ship to come to grief on shore near Scarborough was the 388-ton *Melba*, a three-masted barque owned by

Messrs Tate & Co. of Newcastle. She was towed into the South Bay by a pleasure steamer after experiencing difficulties in heavy seas on 24 June 1919.

The *Melba* was anchored in the bay where she prepared to ride out the storm. However, conditions worsened and at ten o'clock that night distress signals from the *Melba* were seen on shore and the lifeboat was launched. The eight crew members were taken off and landed safely while the barque was left to the mercy of the seas. All night she lay at anchor but at 10 am next day she was seen to be dragging across the bay swaying drunkenly as the seas battered her hull.

Slowly but surely she was driven towards the angry rocks that flank White Nab where she finally stranded and was smashed to pieces by the surf. The *Melba* had been *en route* for Blyth from Treport, France, under the command of Captain Robert C. Roberts.

During the summer of 1971 divers found large pintles from the rudder of a sailing vessel in Cornelian Bay, south of White Nab. It is highly likely that these are relics of the ill-fated *Melba*.

Many vessels of all types have foundered at sea off Scarborough for all sorts of reasons, ranging from sheer unseaworthiness to enemy action.

Bad weather has also played a large part in the toll, as in the case of the 409-ton screw steamer *Glengarry*, bound for Rotterdam from Grangemouth with a cargo of refuse chemicals. At 4 am on Friday, 15 February 1884, she was caught by a south-easterly gale which was to seal her fate. She smashed her way through the mounting waves with impunity for five hours, until a particularly heavy sea struck her broadside on and her cargo shifted. Desperately the crew began to dump ten tons of chemicals overboard, but her dangerous list could not be corrected and distress signals were hoisted which were seen from Scarborough. Two tugs went off to aid her while the rescue services were got ready.

The crew of the *Glengarry* could not wait however. The port lifeboat was lowered and two men clambered aboard. The lifeboat capsized at once, but they were able to cling to the boat until the yawl *Ruby* came up and saved them.

The ship's engineers were less fortunate. They abandoned the steamer in the jolly boat, which also capsized, drowning both of them.

Captain Menzies and the remaining five crew members were struggling to launch the starboard lifeboat as the *Glengarry* settled lower in the water but they could not free it. Fortunately, the steam trawler *Flying Sprite* was alongside by this time, and ropes were thrown to the *Glengarry*. The survivors leapt over the side and were hauled through the icy sea to safety. Seven minutes after the last man left, the vessel was seen to founder.

Backhouse and Dixon had built the *Glengarry* in 1865 and she was owned by J. M. Lennard & Son of Middlesbrough,.

Collisions at sea have also been a major cause of shipping losses off Scarborough, usually as a result of bad visibility particularly in fog.

One such victim was the 714-ton *Haswell*, a steam collier owned by J. Fenwick & Son of London. She was bound for London from Sunderland on Friday, 21 September 1888, when dense fog came down, and she collided with the *SS Vinomona* off Scarborough. The *Haswell* sank quickly, but her crew were picked up by the badly damaged *Vinomona*, which landed them at Sunderland early on Saturday morning.

Built in 1861 by J. Laing of Sunderland, the *Haswell* was made of iron and rigged as a three-masted schooner.

A few weeks later on 27 October 1888, another collision occurred off the town, but for a very different reason. A strong gale was blowing and two sailing vessels, the schooners *Emily Ann*, of Poole and *Queen of Ipswich*, were both tacking south. Suddenly the wheel chain of the *Emily Ann* snapped, rendering her helpless. She strove towards the *Queen* and, striking her amidships, cut her to the water line.

Three of the crew of the *Queen*, realising that their ship was doomed, leapt over the side and grasped the bowsprit of the *Emily Ann* in order to save themselves. The master and mate of the *Queen* were aft at the time of the collision and before they could scramble forward their vessel had drifted astern of the *Emily Ann*. The *Queen* foundered, taking Captain Alf Osborne and the mate with her.

Owned by Alfred Beaumont of Ipswich, the *Queen* was a 109-tons gross vessel, built fifty years earlier by Bayley, of Ipswich.

Reference has already been made to the large number of sailing craft that were little better than floating coffins because they were dangerously unseaworthy. It is easy to understand why a vessel might founder in storm-tossed seas, but when a ship sank on a flat calm day, that vessel surely ought never to have put to sea.

The last days of the brigantine *Star of the West* serve to illustrate clearly why sailing colliers were regarded by seamen as the lowest form of craft afloat. On 30 March 1892 this wretched vessel left the Tyne with 348 tons of coal bound for Jersey, under Captain H. Saunders and seven hands.

When she sailed there were several inches of water swilling about in the bottom of the vessel, but this was not considered to be important.

Between nine and ten o'clock that night, when the brigantine was some thirty-five miles east of Scarborough, it was found that the water level had risen alarmingly and all hands were ordered to the pumps. The water continued to gain on them however, until it reached a depth of eleven and then fifteen feet.

All hope of saving the *Star of the West* was abandoned and the crew calmly prepared to leave her. They launched the longboat and remained alongside until the vessel settled at 6 am, head foremost, in a very calm sea.

The skipper of the Scarborough trawler *Lord Clyde* saw the brigantine sinking and steamed up to it, took the crew aboard and landed them at Scarborough.

Later in the morning the *SS Dalhousie* picked up the jolly boat belonging to the brigantine so that both the vessel's boats were saved.

The *Star of the West*, 211-ton gross, was owned by J. Dorey and Co. of Guernsey and had been built there in 1869. She had originally been employed in the West Indies and South American trade.

At midnight on 4 August 1914, Britain declared war on Germany and four months later, on 16 December, Scarborough suffered what was described as "England's first direct experience of the greatest war of all time". A German battle-cruiser squadron shelled the town for a period of nearly twenty minutes, in which time 16 people were killed and many more were wounded. What was not immediately obvious was that the bombardment was carried out partly as a cover for the German light-cruiser *Kolberg*, which laid a hundred mines close inshore between Scarborough and Filey.

British warships immediately set out to engage the enemy fleet, and one theory is that the German ships were hoping to lure the British fleet into their minefield.

Had this manoeuvre succeeded, the result would have been disastrous for Great Britain, but fortunately the weather intervened. A thick mist descended, reducing visibility to a few thousand yards, and the opposing fleets lost contact with each other. The Scarborough minefield proved to be frighteningly effective. Within ten days it caused the loss of eight steamships and three naval trawlers. Several other ships were severely damaged.

One of the early victims, the steamer *Elterwater*, had left the Tyne that morning with coal for London. At 6.10 pm she struck one of the Kolberg's mines three miles off shore and sank within three minutes, giving the crew no time to launch their lifeboats. Captain David Gillan and the seventeen crew swam around amid the wreckage, clinging to anything that would float. Twelve of them were eventually picked up by boats from the steamer *City of Newcastle*, which had been abreast of the *Elterwater* when she struck the mine, but six men had already died.

The second mate, John Leakin, died later from injuries received and an inquest was held six days later.

The *Elterwater* was a 1,228-ton steamer owned by the Sharp Steam Ship Co. and built by the Blyth Shipbuilding Co. in 1907.

Two other vessels sank as a result of striking the mines on the same day, 16 December 1914. They were the 1,090-ton *Vaaren*, a new Norwegian vessel, and the 988-ton *Princess Olga*, owned by M. Langland & Sons of Liverpool and Glasgow.

As a result of these losses, the Admiralty instructed Hull trawlers to suspend fishing operations until the minefield had been swept.

Early on the morning of 19 December 1914 a fleet of mine sweeping trawlers steamed past Filey in line ahead toward Scarborough. They had been ordered to clear the minefield, and were now speeding towards the danger area pouring volumes of dense black smoke into the clear sunlit sky.

Lieutenant Godfrey Parsons, a retired naval officer, was commanding the squadron from his 'flagship', the trawler *Passing*.

Six miles seaward, three old gunboats were already engaged in the deadly work of sweeping the mines. These were the *Skipjack*, *Jason* and *Gossamer*, bound for Scapa Flow from Sheerness, when they received orders to assist the minesweeping trawlers. As the mines were anchored to the seabed, they were much nearer to the surface when the tide was at its lowest ebb. Consequently the minesweepers had orders to suspend operations for two hours either side of low water.

The work began at about 8.30 am and for a time all went well. The sweeps cut through the mines' anchors and, more often than not, also detonated them. Those that did not explode were broken free whence they rose to the surface and were detonated by gunfire. In this way eighteen mines were quickly disposed of, but no-one then knew that such a large number of the deadly things were to be found.

Before long dreadful confusion resulted; minesweepers with their sweeps tangled or parted were intermingled with floating mines as the tide dropped rapidly.

The inevitable happened. The 273-ton *Orianda* struck a mine while steaming full ahead and blew her bows to pieces. Unable to stop, she steamed beneath the surface until nothing remained but her masthead, cutting through the water like a submarine periscope.

Surprisingly, only one man died in the blast; the rest escaped with their lives, including Lt. H. B. Boothby, her commander who was subsequently given command of the *Banyers*, another minesweeper. Within a few weeks was mined again in the same area.

A second trawler, the *Passing*, was blown up with the loss of one life but she was towed into Scarborough (Figure 3).

Fig. 3: The bows of the steam trawler *Passing*
after striking a mine in December 1914.

At this the senior officer ordered that the squadron should anchor where they were and wait for the tide to rise again.

The following day, 20 December, the 203-ton auxiliary patrol trawler *Garmo* was mined and sunk off Scarborough with the loss of six lives, one of which was the skipper, T. Gilbert. Nine of her survivors were picked up by the drifter *Principal*.

On the same day the armed yacht *Valiant* was severely damaged by a mine, but she too was safely brought into harbour.

On 22 December the 1,168-ton Norwegian steamer *Boston* struck a mine, but did not sink at once. She drifted south and struck Filey Brigg where she sank without loss of life. Capt. A. J. Olsen and the eighteen crew were saved by the lifeboat.

Perhaps the cruellest blow of all was that which struck on Christmas Day when three vessels went to the bottom as a result of the *Kolberg's* mines. The 1,107-ton Norwegian steamer *Eli*, from Blyth with coal, went down within three minutes of the impact, yet her fifteen crew were all saved.

During the summer of 1971, divers found the wreck of the *Eli* in some 75 feet of water off Redcliff, three miles south of Scarborough. Though badly broken up, parts of her were still clearly recognisable. The bow section was almost intact except for a gaping hole on her port side which was probably caused by the mine.

Built in 1870 by Bergens Mek Voerks, the *Eli* was owned by Peder Lindoe of Haugesund. She now lies in position 54° 15' 20" N 0° 18' 00" W.

Close by lies the wreck of the *Gem*, a 446-ton steamer owned by Robertsons of Glasgow and mined on the same day as the *Eli*. The *Gem* went down with the loss of her captain and nine crew.

The third loss on this awful day was the minesweeping trawler *Nighthawk*, a Grimsby vessel of 287-tons that also fell foul of the Scarborough minefield. Six of her crew were lost but seven others survived, largely thanks to the efforts of the skipper, Lt. W. E. Senior, who sculled round on a life raft picking up his ship-mates. It was freezing hard at the time, a strong wind was blowing and the water was icy cold.

Within a month, 53 mines had been swept up, but the carnage continued for some time after this.

The sweeping ended on 23 April 1915, by which time 69 mines had been swept and several more had already served their purpose.

All told the Scarborough minefield caused the loss of over 100 lives. Seven British merchant steamers, seven neutrals, two trawlers and four minesweepers, and many other vessels were seriously damaged.

Never again in the whole course of the war were mines laid so thickly in any part of the world.

It should be recorded here that during World War I no less than 214 minesweepers were sunk, roughly one per week for the whole period of war. Each time one of these vessels was mined, on average half of the crew were lost.

MINE SWEEPER DAMAGED BY MINE LEFT BY GERMANS AFTER THE RAID ON DEC. 16ᵗʰ 1914.

Fig. 4: A minesweeper damaged by a mine
laid by the Germans on 16 December 1914.

A new and even more frightening menace appeared before the last mine was destroyed: the enemy submarine.

Eight steamers became victims of the U-boat attacks off Scarborough during the war with the loss of many men.

On 13 March 1915 the 1,573-ton Swedish steamer *Hanna* was off Scarborough, bound for Las Palmas with coal from the Tyne.

Shortly after midnight the Second Officer was on watch when he saw what appeared to be the wash of a torpedo on the star-board side. An explosion followed which blew away much of the stem of the vessel, killing six of the eight men sleeping in the foc'sle.

The vessel began to sink at once and the crew took to the boats. Fourteen of them were landed at Hull by the steamer *Gylier*.

The significant feature of this disaster was that the *Hanna* was a neutral vessel. Her name and nationality were painted clearly on the ship's side in large letters.

The German policy of sinking all vessels in the North Sea did not begin for some time after this event, but it seemed clear that the *Hanna* was the victim of a torpedo rather than a mine.

Too often the U-boats escaped unscathed after they had succeeded in sinking their victims, but occasionally the hunter became the hunted.

On 10 August 1918 the UB-30 torpedoed and sank the 509-ton *Madame Renee* off Scarborough early in the morning. The local lifeboat went to the scene of the disaster and picked up two survivors. Four more had been taken aboard the passing cargo vessel *Tynesider*, but the remaining ten men had died.

Three days later the UB-30 was sunk off Whitby while she was preparing to strike again.

She was not the first U-boat to sink here however. On 4 October 1917 watchers at Scarborough had seen an offshore explosion marking, it was thought, the end of UB-41 which had been operating in the area.

It was not certain whether she had struck British mines laid early in September, or German ones laid on July 9 by UB-55, another enemy mine-laying submarine.

By the time the war ended, sailing vessels were becoming rare off the Yorkshire coast and, as steamers were less vulnerable, the number of shipping losses dropped dramatically.

The most serious hazard was still the weather, though fog was now feared more than gales. Radar had not yet been thought of and, while captains stood a better chance of weathering storms in their larger and more powerful vessels, they were just as vulnerable as they had always been when visibility dropped.

On 8 July 1927 the small coaster *Westowrie* passed Scarborough *en route* for Yarmouth with stone from Inverkeithing. Thick fog blanketed the coast and Captain Allen, who was also part owner, peered anxiously into the gloom.

Suddenly, at 6.45 am, another steamer, the *Lambeth*, loomed out of the fog on a collision course and the *Westowrie* frantically sounded her siren.

Fig. 5: The keelboat *Sincere* stranded south of Cayton Bay where she became a wreck, May 1968.

The master of the *Lambeth* returned the signal and put his engines hard astern. But it was too late. The vessels collided stem-to-stem with a sickening crunch, and almost immediately drew apart and lost each other in the fog.

The *Lambeth* stopped engines and all hands peered into the fog, straining their eyes and ears for any sign of the other vessel. They could hear and see nothing and after some time cautiously resumed their passage for the Tyne with a slightly damaged bow.

The *Westowrie* in fact was in real trouble. Her bows were stove in and she was taking water rapidly. Captain Allen and the five crew abandoned ship and when the fog lifted slightly were spotted and taken aboard a passing steamer, the *Chartered*, bound for Newcastle.

The *Westowrie* sank some four hours after the collision.

Fortunately, World War II brought no repetition of the 1914-18 dramas, but it did add one new form of disaster to the terrible list.

On 16 October 1940, the 25-ton fishing vessel *Pride of Scarborough* struck a mine that had been dropped by parachute from a German aircraft. She was blown to pieces just outside the harbour mouth. All her crew were lost in the disaster.

Another mine claimed the last vessel to be wrecked here two years after hostilities had ceased.

On 7 October 1947 an explosion shook the town with such violence that observers thought the lighthouse pier was going to collapse. Mariners knew only too well the sound of an exploding mine, and a fleet of fishing vessels steamed out to render what assistance they could.

The victim was the 1,771-ton collier *Betty Hindley*, mined at 9.10 am some three miles north of the town. Distress signals on the siren guided the would-be-rescuers to the vessel that was settling by the bow.

Tow ropes were connected to her stern and the little fleet began the long haul to the South Bay.

Their efforts were to no avail. In spite of the help of tugboats, the next day the vessel foundered some three-quarters of a mile from the harbour mouth where she became a total wreck.

In the blast one man had been killed and two others, one of them Captain Cole, were severely injured.

The *Betty Hindley*, owned by Stephenson Clarke of London, was subsequently dispersed by salvage contractors, but today the wreck site is still a favourite for local divers.

The bows are intact, rising some 25 feet from the seabed, and fish swim lazily in and out of the gaping hole left by the explosion.

Trawlers in Scarborough Harbour.